THE PRAETORIAN GUARD:

The U.S. Role in the New World Order

THE PRAETORIAN GUARD:

The U.S. Role in the New World Order

John Stockwell

Editing, design, and production by the South End Press
collective
Cover by Nancy Adams

Library of Congress Cataloging-in-Publication Data

Stockwell, John, 1937-
    The Praetorian guard : the U.S. role in the new world
order / by John Stockwell.
    p. cm.
    Essays based on earlier lectures.
    Includes bibliographical references and index.
  ISBN 0-89608-396-9 : $30.00. -- ISBN 0-89608-395-0 (pbk.) : $11.00
    1. United States--Politics and government--1945- 2. United
States--Military relations--Foreign countries. I. Title.
E839.5.S78   1991   90-27481
322'.5'0973--dc20   CIP

South End Press, 116 St. Botolph St., Boston, MA 02115

99 98 97 96 95 94 93 92 91   1 2 3 4 5 6 7 8 9

TABLE OF CONTENTS

FOOTNOTES / 147

AUTHOR'S NOTE

This book was made possible by the joint efforts of several dedicated individuals. For years I had tried, unsuccessfully, to obtain a grant that would enable me to produce a more formal and somewhat longer study of the complex subject of national and world security, of the engines that drive the United States into overt and covert war. I had all but given up on rendering in print the material I had discussed in so many lectures when Michelle Michael Reel transcribed presentations I had made in the House of Commons in London and at American University, where I caused a stir by predicting the December 1989 invasion of Panama, a prediction that was replayed on C-SPAN.

Bill Fason, Ben Moss, and Greg Roberts reworked the text repeatedly. Ellen Herman, my editor at South End Press, undertook the challenge of transforming and reorganizing the lectures into a book. Peter Solomon's keen eye was invaluable. Obviously I pitched in, revising and updating until early December 1990.

Who knows? Perhaps the result will be more useful to busy people at 200 pages than it would have been at 600! We certainly hope so. The issues could not be clearer or more vital as the nation prepares for war in the Persian Gulf, while the economy faces a grim reckoning, and the President seems to look to the interests of the "new world order," as he calls it, more eagerly than to those of the American people.

This book deals with today's problems, extensively citing the current President, George Bush. However, the thesis presented here was formulated in the 1970s and early 1980s, long before Bush was elected to the presidency. I managed the CIA's Angola Task Force in 1976, when George Bush was Director of the CIA. As you will read below, our impression at the time was that he was a bright, conscientious person, a nice man, who was considerate to his subordinates. It is his policies as Vice-President, then President, that trouble me.

To assist and encourage the reader to pursue the many subjects taken up in this book, a lengthy annotated bibliography is provided at the end. Approximately 120 of the best books on national and world security are listed, organized by subject, most with a brief comment to facilitate one's choice. (Some of the annotations include material—for example, about AIDS, the "Magic Bullet," KAL 007, Nugan-Hand Bank, and Bobby Kennedy's death—that is not included in the text.)

I urge everyone to read and judge for themselves. I claim that our leaders systematically misrepresent the facts and mislead us about their intentions. Some of their deceptions, especially if you are young, may encourage you to go off some day and be killed, or to kill others. These are serious charges: our leaders lie to us for greedy, selfish, and deadly purposes. Obviously I could be dead wrong. That's what democracy is really about, or at least should be about: reading, reflecting, and deciding.

The French have a saying, *Ceux qui ne font pas la politique seront fait.* Those who do not do politics will be done.

Humans are programmable creatures. We are conditioned from childhood to perceptions and beliefs that influence our reactions for the rest of our lives. As a result, we can respond to stirring rhetoric, even to the point of marching off to war or shrugging off concerns about the pollution of the world's ecosystem. As a young man, knowing very little about the world, I took up the call to arms, and my family was proud. So did Daniel Ellsberg, Gore Vidal, Bo Gritz, Brian Willson, and literally millions of others over the years. Many did not survive the experience.

My point is this: if you do not defend yourself with knowledge, others can and will pick your pocket and use you to their own advantage.

THE SCOPE OF THE PROBLEM

In the spring of 1977, having just served on a subcommittee of the National Security Council as chief of the CIA's Angola Task Force, I left the CIA. I was determined to testify to the congressional oversight committees about the laws we had broken in Angola, and I did. I also wrote a book on the subject, *In Search of Enemies* (New York, Norton 1978), whose title outlined a useful thesis that would be echoed in other books and even such conservative publications as *Time Magazine.* Soon I launched myself on a long and persistent reading-and-traveling self-education program about the Cold War in which I had been a soldier. My first lectures were appropriately called "The Secret Wars of the CIA."

In time, I met intellectual leaders and critics of the nuclear arms race like Carl Sagan, Admiral Gene LaRocque of the Center for Defense Information, and Helen Caldicott of Physicians for Social Responsibility. I devoured book after book on the subject and I began to offer in my lectures an explanation of how the CIA's covert activities, its "secret wars," related to the arms race. What did President Reagan's *contra* destabilization of Nicaragua have to do with the massive $2.5 trillion military buildup he supervised in the 1980s?

Then in 1989, the Cold War came to an abrupt halt as the Soviet Union admitted its bankruptcy, the Soviet Bloc was set free, and the Berlin Wall dismantled. In a worldwide atmosphere of celebration, I found myself accused of compulsive cynicism when I expressed skepticism that the dawn of an era of freedom had come. I, and of course thousands of others, set about watching and analyzing the post-Cold War world. Would the giant military complexes be dismantled? Would violent covert activities that had been justified in the name of anti-Communism be curtailed? Would the tightening fist of national security laws and restrictions be relaxed? Would powerful political and economic elites willingly release their accumulated power? Or would new rationales be found for profitable old policies?

It seemed apparent that the United States and the Soviet Union had both lost the Cold War. Because of over-commitment to the production of arms and the maintenance of vast military forces, each emerged with permanently damaged economies, neither in control of their economic futures. Instead, the winners of the Cold War were, ironically enough, Japan and Germany, the vanquished losers of World War II, countries that had been prohibited from major investments in the production of arms and hence were forced to turn to trade goods instead.

Both the United States and the Soviet Union, however, remain military superpowers, locked in a symbiotic union of muscle and money with the world's transnational bankers. They are, especially the United States, the "Praetorian Guard" of the new world order.[1]

We now live in the Age of *Glasnost* with an ex-CIA Director as President of the United States and an ex-KGB official as President of the Soviet Union. Mikhail Gorbachev offers policies of openness; George Bush came into office promising a kinder, gentler United States that would project a thousand points of light. They have assured us that the Cold War is over, as they advertise their personal friendship. This process began formally in 1988, when President Ronald Reagan and Chairman Mikhail Gorbachev came together in Washington and Moscow to sign the Intermediate Nuclear Forces (INF) Treaty and spoke of eliminating all strategic nuclear weapons by the end of the century. It culminated in November 1990 when Presidents Bush and Gorbachev, and leaders of seventeen countries met to sign the papers that would disassemble much of the Cold War apparatus in Europe.

Unfortunately, however, our world is still fraught with grievous problems. In December 1989, the United States invaded Panama in an expensive, bloody, and pointless invasion to capture General Manuel Noriega, who will probably never be brought to trial, at least not to a remotely fair trial. Bush has continued President Reagan's expensive militarist programs and the massive assault on domestic social programs. As I write this, he is in the Persian Gulf, reviewing U.S. troops on the eve of what promises to be an expensive, bloody war against Iraq.

On the other side of the great ocean, Soviet President Gorbachev is trying desperately to keep the USSR from splintering into fifteen republics (each, as he has warned, potentially in possession of nuclear capabilities) and a half-dozen civil wars. While advocating commendable openness and tolerance, he has in fact consolidated his presidential powers and has not hesitated to order his troops to gun down rioting protestors. As millions of people face possible food shortages in the coming winter, he probably has much more prestige overseas than he does at home.

The Soviet peoples may have been sold a package of illusions to justify the country's ideological surrender to the West. Because their own system clearly wasn't working, it was easy to dream that conversion to free market capitalism would bring quick prosperity. The word "profit" seemed to mean "open sesame." But it isn't that simple. The Soviet Union's problems are ingrained in institutions that have evolved over many decades and they won't be resolved quickly, or even in a few years. For example, how effective is freedom of the press if one congested government bureaucracy controls the distribution of all paper and ink?

Meanwhile, our planet is still booby-trapped with 60,000 thermonuclear weapons, and our factories are still producing, testing, and developing new systems. In the 1980s, the United States indulged itself in a $2.5 trillion spending spree—and that is a conservative, published figure—the largest peacetime arms buildup in the history of the world. Not coincidentally, the U.S. national debt was increased by about the same amount, to its present level of about $4 trillion. In the 1970s, the United States was the richest country in the world. We had not been a debtor nation since before World War I. Now we have the greatest debt in the history of the world, with a deficit that is running over $1 billion each day, $385 billion per year.

Within the parameters of the militarist economy, there is no solution to this economic *zugswang,* to the huge debt and the continuing deficits that profoundly threaten our economic strength now and in the future. The President's vacillating anguish during the budgetary process in September 1990 would have brought down the government of a parliamentary system like England's. Even during the spring of 1990, columnists began to write that he was destined to be a one-term president.

The United States maintains, after the announced end of the Cold War, an open policy of supporting coups, destabilizations, and "violent low-intensity conflicts" in every corner of the globe. The secret wars of the CIA continued unabated.

U.S. society is said to be drowning in a sea of drugs and an official Drug Czar is engaged in a "war" against the criminal czars. This war was been used to justify the invasion of Panama and significant changes in the U.S. legal system in favor of secrecy and arbitrary governmental power at the expense of civil liberties. Integral to the other broad problems facing our society —the collapse of the U.S. economy, the arms race, the CIA's secret wars—is the systematic destruction of our environment, a seemingly inherent characteristic of the military-industrial complex.

The U.S. leadership is faced with a stirring and awakening of the American people to the cynicism with which their pockets have been picked while their social services have been curtailed to a point far below that of other industrial nations. People are recognizing the long-term damage that has been done to the nation's economy and to the environment. They are growing restless. Historically, this has been the setting in which our leaders have turned to dramatic foreign adventures that will distract the people. Faced with similar crises in the past, our leaders have, time and time again, taken the nation to war.

In 1897, Theodore Roosevelt wrote to a friend: "In strict confidence...I should welcome almost any war, for I think this country needs one."[2] We know how these ingredients work. Our history is clear to all who can or will make the time to read the books that are now available. In spring 1989, I was able to predict the invasion of Panama nine months before it happened. In the winter and spring of 1990, I was able to predict that the U.S. leadership would have to conjure up a war before 1992 to distract the people from the domestic problems facing the nation, and from our leaders' cynical failure. The U.S. national security establishment was targeting Cuba, "the last redoubt of

Stalinism," as they called it, and its embattled leader, Fidel Castro.

In August 1990, by invading Kuwait, Saddam Hussein gave the U.S. President the remarkable gift of a golden opportunity for bold military action. President Bush seized the opportunity and rushed hundreds of thousands of troops to the area. None of this was accidental. Admiral Eugene Carroll Jr. of the Center for Defense Information observes that the U.S. is not in fact dealing with a "crisis" in the Persian Gulf. Rather, Admiral Carroll notes, the White House has engineered a *casus belli,* a situation regarded as justifying war. Through Kuwait, the CIA has been destabilizing Iraq. During the Iran/Iraq war of the 1980s, Kuwait advanced its border further north and seized valuable Iraqi oil reserves. By manipulating oil prices, Kuwait cost Iraq billions of dollars in revenues. Meanwhile, on the eve of Iraq's invasion of Kuwait, the U.S. ambassador gave Saddam Hussein what seemed to be tacit reassurance that the United States would not respond.

Had Hussein asked me, I would have assured him with confidence that President Bush would respond vigorously. President Bush was shopping around for a war.

The Persian Gulf crisis has provided a graphic lesson in the rationales of the new world security complex in the post-Cold War era. In the spring and summer of 1990, the military establishment that President Dwight D. Eisenhower dubbed the "military industrial complex" thirty-odd years ago was faced with a massive cutback of its budgets and influence. (Note that this is now a *world* military order, as the defense corporations and the bankers that finance them are transnational conglomerates.) There was even excited talk of a great peace dividend from the cessation of Cold War hostilities.

After Iraq's invasion of Kuwait, newspapers ran several pages each day about the crisis and all its ramifications, complete with photographs of George Bush on his golf cart and fishing boat at his Maine home. President Bush brilliantly manipulated the Persian Gulf crisis into a "WIN/WIN" situation, at least in his interests. The nation has already forgotten the budget and deficits crisis of September, and there is no more talk of the President's

vacillating leadership, whose only consistent feature was devoted service to the ultra-rich. Very little space has been left in
the media for the Savings and Loan scandal. The newspapers
are bursting with Christmas sympathy for our boys (many of
whom may soon die) in the Gulf—how to write them letters,
how to send them cookies—instead of dwelling on the collap-
sing job and real estate markets.

The rationales for a war in the Persian Gulf are so solid that
even the Democratic Congress apparently feels obliged to support President Bush's Middle East initiatives, and he has been
able to weave together a broad international coalition behind
sanctions against Iraq. On his way to Helsinki to discuss
planned military action with Mikhail Gorbachev, Bush announced, *"We now have the opportunity to establish a new world
order."* By the end of 1990, President Bush had achieved broad
support, even from the United Nations, for military action—
war—against Iraq.

A new world order? In whose interests? His own? The
American people's?

The cynicism of the President's Persian Gulf policies is
demonstrable and breath-taking. Looking directly into television cameras he has said, "Surely there is no one in this nation
so cynical they would believe I would play politics with our
boys' lives in the Persian Gulf," precisely at the moment when
he was playing politics with their lives. The impending war was
first justified by the necessity of low-cost gasoline. Yet prices
jumped in the service stations because of greedy speculation
and months later, there is still no shortage of oil. President Bush
is an oil-man, and one of his sons has substantial investments
in Middle Eastern oil. The week before Iraq's invasion of Kuwait, the Senate Armed Services Committee voted unanimously
to cut the expensive, ineffective B-2 Stealth bomber; the week
after, the body of the Senate voted to restore it. Within six weeks,
President Bush announced that the Persian Gulf crisis justified
the full restoration of the Stealth bomber, the Star Wars program,
and other strategic missiles and systems.

Meanwhile, the military establishment, of which the president is both the commander-in-chief and the spiritual leader,

has used the Persian Gulf situation successfully to restore its budgets—to an all time high of over $300 billion—and abolish any thought of a peace dividend, but also to recast its rationales for continuing dominance of U.S. society. The Soviet Union's leader is now cooperating with and supporting U.S. policies. The new threat to U.S. national security is now said to lie in the Third World where countries like Iraq have sizeable armies and are developing nuclear capabilities.

The military spending that has put the U.S. economy into such a deep hole promises to continue apace and the repressive national security laws to continue to devour the Bill of Rights, while the United States protects the interests of the financial order that dominates the world of today and of the foreseeable future.

If Saddam Hussein withdraws from Kuwait, Bush will stand very tall, taking credit for bluffing the man down. War is good business and, if done properly and under the right circumstances, good politics. Even without a violent conflict, the President has accomplished a great deal in his own and in the military establishment's interests.

At the same time, Bush has dealt the nation a "LOSE/LOSE" hand in the Persian Gulf. He has painted himself into a corner. Should Hussein not withdraw, he will have no choice but to go to war, whether or not the country supports him. Even with the quick military victory he promises, the body bags will come home and the nation will not be denied the post mortem: Why did we do this? Was it worth it? We will want to know if jobs are restored, if gasoline prices go down, and if stability is achieved in the Middle East. The U.S. budget and deficit problems will not go away. The cost of the war itself and the reaffirmation of the United States as a permanent war complex will exacerbate the nation's problems and insure the United States' continuing economic decline.

It is fascinating to watch as President Bush encounters opposition to war in the Persian Gulf from the commandant of the Marine Corps, the commander of U.S. forces in the Persian Gulf, two former chairmen of the Joint Chiefs of Staff, and other heavyweights in the military establishment. With the military budget suddenly restored to an all-time high, could it be that some of the military planners are not eager to provoke the nation with the slaughter of thousands? In a similar situation in the 1980s, the Pentagon successfully resisted President Reagan's and Secretaries of State George Schultz's and Al Haig's efforts to invade Nicaragua and to "go to the source" in Cuba. Nevertheless, the military's pursuit of bloated budgets is irresponsible.

The US. budget and deficit problems will not go away. The cost of placing 400,000 U.S. troops in the Gulf and the reaffirmation of the U.S. extravagant and permanent war complex will exacerbate the nation's problems and insure continuing decline.

Of course, President Bush might play the war-card yet again. Cuba is standing by, ever the defiant, designated enemy of the United States, against whose leaders George Bush has sworn unbending antipathy.

Without war in the Persian Gulf, there will be no opportunity to destroy Iraq's nuclear capability—a primary objective of powerful lobbies in the United States. However, Richard Rhodes, whose highly acclaimed book, *The Making of the Atomic Bomb,* is the definitive work on the subject, noted in the *New York Times* that Iraq is in fact ten years away from a functional bomb (light years from one with a delivery system that could reach the United States) and that, historically, acquiring a nuclear capability has had a stabilizing influence on other combative adventurers because it then makes them nuclear targets. Both Iraq and Israel will be given pause, when considering military activity in the Middle East, precisely because of their nuclear weapons.

That is what this book is all about: why the United States regularly goes to war; why it so eagerly rushed its troops into the Persian Gulf in August 1990, into Panama in December 1989, and into Vietnam after the Gulf of Tonkin incident in 1965; why a war in the Middle East would be a long-term disaster. How do CIA activities, the environment, and the economy tie into this war compulsion? What is at stake in terms of *real* national security interests and for freedom and democracy in the "new world order"?

EX-CIA DIRECTOR,
PRESIDENT GEORGE BUSH

The infamous case of Manuel Noriega illustrates the liability the United States now bears by having an ex-CIA Director as president. Manuel Noriega, who, according to President Bush was a paid CIA agent under six presidents, boasted in 1988 that "I have George Bush by the balls."[3]

There are Noriegas all over the world, unsavory characters who have smuggled drugs and conducted illegal operations. Any CIA Director is inevitably dirtied by association with such people, and they would know things about him that could be very politically damaging. Surely, this kind of knowledge must influence numerous policy decisions. Noriega fell out with the CIA, flaunted his knowledge of secrets, and paid a grave price for it in December 1989, when the United States invaded Panama and brought Noriega to the United States, supposedly to stand trial. So did the thousands of Panamanian people who were wounded and killed in the invasion.

President Bush, who campaigned on the promise of a "kinder and gentler" United States, is the same person who authorized the CIA to spend about $10 million to rig the elections in Panama in May 1989. After two botched coup attempts, Bush finally orchestrated public opinion against Noriega sufficiently to order the full invasion of Panama.

George Bush, the politician, benefited from that invasion. With great élan, like a 19th-century British lord, he went dove-hunting while U.S. troops blasted Panama, once and for all erasing the stigma of wimpiness that has haunted his political life. Let his enemies know and be afraid!

Another advantage of the Panama operation was the useful political distraction it provided although there wasn't yet a broad realization that the U.S. economy was in dire shape and heading downward. Short, successful military adventures are as effective as the Super Bowl in diverting people's attention from unpleasant truths.

I worked for George Bush at the end of the Angolan operation when he was CIA Director in 1976. Like the Iran/*contra* team afterwards, and many others before us, we had broken various laws and we had perjured ourselves to cover it up—"we" being Secretary of State Henry Kissinger and CIA Director William Colby, with people like myself in staff positions supporting them. Bush's policy was *not* to investigate, *not* to dig out the truth, and *not* to punish the perpetrators in order to discipline and clean up the CIA. His policy was to cover up for us. He called it "restoring the CIA's morale." Director Bush went to the congressional committees that were investigating the Angola operation and said, "I wasn't here when the Angola thing happened, but these nice people I'm meeting out at CIA Headquarters in Langley, I can't believe they would really do the things you are alleging. I promise I will investigate personally."

Inside the CIA, Bush came across as a very nice person. Most CIA directors walk around a little somber, and you don't mess with them. Bush was a contrast; he was a politician. He would walk down the hall shaking our hands, saying, "Hello, I am George Bush and I want you to know I love being here working with all these fine people in the CIA." "Huh?" we said. I mean this was the CIA *Director.* We saw him as fluff. There were a lot of jokes.

In retrospect, I realize that we were fooled. Bush was carefully building relationships in the CIA underworld that would continue when he became Vice-President and then President. New CIA friends, like Donald Gregg, would join his Vice-Presidential staff, then go on to ambassadorial appointments. They would be sprinkled throughout high offices in the Bush presidency, giving the intelligence community, with all its cynical ethos, enormous influence on the U.S. government and national policy.

These contacts were incidental, however, to Bush's broader plan. He used his position as CIA director to bring into the agency a team of right-wing economists who would cook the statistical books and publish a bloated assessment of alleged military spending by the Soviet Union. Their report was the basis of Bush's run for the presidency in 1980, and for the dramatic and successful bid by the military establishment for the huge arms buildup of the 1980s. Ironically, the more strident and charismatic Ronald Reagan preempted Bush's platform and stole the Republican Party nomination from George Bush in 1980. As Machiavelli taught, politicians are partly the victims of chance, while they plot to advance their interests.

At the time of the 1980 election campaign, Bush was more moderate than Ronald Reagan, and was obliged to serve eight years as Vice-President. He used the time well; he worked quietly with the U.S. secret government, the "secret team," in drug, terrorist, and Iran/*contra* activities, building contacts throughout the national and world security complexes. He became one of the key players in the Reagan Revolution.

That revolution may have been misunderstood and underestimated by many Americans. President Reagan and his revolutionaries were not mincing words. They intended to effect a permanent *revolutionary* change to the U.S. system of government. They planned to catch the pendulum as it swung to the right and weld it in place, where it could never swing back to the left. Like committed revolutionaries, they were profoundly irreverent of sacred institutions.

Reagan's first term in office was deliberately provocative. He preached that nuclear war was survivable; that we might drop "demonstration" weapons on Europe to intimidate the Soviets. He joked (once accidentally, on a live radio show) that he had already launched U.S. missiles against the Soviet Union. Jerry Falwell, who preached that nuclear Armageddon might be God's instrument for taking his chosen up on high, was a regular visitor to the White House. Reagan was openly contemptuous of environmental concerns: "If you've seen one redwood you've seen them all." He appointed James Watt, who systematically opened millions of acres of government land to commercial exploitation, to the Interior Department and Ann Burford, who used the Environmental Protection Agency (EPA) to protect corporations that were dumping and poisoning.

Reagan willfully assaulted the human services infrastructure in the United States, boasting that he had eliminated over 1000 programs that served lower income groups. He proposed that ketchup and pickle relish would suffice for vegetables in school lunches. He raised taxes for the poor and middle class while slashing them by 60 percent for the ultra-rich.

He put Elliott Abrams into the Human Rights Division of the State Department with orders to dismantle it. The Reagan administration sent the files of confidential testimonials that Pat Derian, under President Jimmy Carter, had accumulated from refugees from repressive countries to the police in those countries. Then the Immigration and Naturalization Services deported the refugees to countries where brutal police were waiting for them at the airports.

President Reagan and his attorney general, Edwin Meese III, whose personal corruption came under investigation, ridiculed the plight of the poor and challenged the Constitution itself, saying that it was only a piece of paper. Meese repeatedly asserted the principle that arrested people were to be considered guilty until proven otherwise. Reagan put his and Meese's California friend Luis Guiffrida in charge of the Federal Emergency Management Agency (FEMA), which laid plans to suspend the Constitution, declare martial law, and intern several hundred thousand people without due process. Secretary of State George Shultz lobbied vigorously (with indirect success) for a *pre-emptive strikes bill* that would give him authority to list "known and suspected terrorists" within the United States who could be attacked and killed by government agents with impunity. Shultz admitted (in a public address in October 25, 1984) that the strikes would take place on the basis of information that would never stand up in a court of law and that innocent people would be killed in the process. He insisted, however, that people listed would not be permitted to sue in court to have their names taken off that list.

Many other laws were passed in favor of the national security complex at the expense of civil liberties. By the end of his eight years in office, President Reagan was also boasting that he had appointed 45 percent of the sitting federal judges. He tacitly encouraged the corruption and irresponsibility that eventually led to the Savings and Loan scandal and to 200 of Reagan's officials being indicted, investigated, or fired for corruption.

Only Ronald Reagan, the "Great Communicator" (also called, by the *Washington Post,* the "Great Prevaricator") could have been such an effective point man for an irresponsible "revolution" that assaulted and violated the most profound U.S. traditions and institutions.

Perhaps inevitably, Reagan's excesses brought down his presidency by the middle of his second term in office. Having done his duty to the establishment, he was stopped in the Iran/*contra* scandal, which was exposed by the media that had created him and made his "revolution" possible. The Iran/*contra* hearings and investigations did not, however, go so far as to threaten impeachment, for the revolutionary gains would have been sacrificed in the process.

Instead, George Bush took up the ball and has run with it. A far more careful and skillful politician than Ronald Reagan, he is taking the revolution to its logical conclusion, consolidating power in what he calls the "new world order."

Years ago, after Bush had assured Congress that he would investigate the CIA's Angola operation, a young attorney was sent down to my office to go through my files and purge them of any documents that would prove exactly what the Congress was accusing us of. Then Bush went back to the committees and testified that no files in the agency corroborated any of the Congressional allegations. Congress dropped its investigation.

Another example of Bush's cover-up skills was the 1976 bombing in Washington, DC that killed Orlando Letelier and Ronnie Moffett. It was done by CIA or former CIA agents working with Chilean DINA agents. George Bush immediately went to the Justice Department and asked them to soft-pedal the "incident" because it involved sensitive national security relationships with other countries—meaning the CIA's close relationship with Chilean President Augusto Pinochet's security service in Chile that was the equivalent of the CIA. A fatal bombing in the U.S. capital was not too much for Bush to hide.

As it turned out, the CIA agents or former agents involved in the bombing had been part of the OPMONGOOSE destabilization of Cuba 15 years earlier. Others from that same group had turned to drug-smuggling and mayhem, that included a string of bombings and murders in Florida and New York. Recall that Orlando Bosch was caught firing a bazooka at a ship coming into the Miami port. Because the operation had begun with the CIA intervening with Florida law enforcement officers, they had been so corrupted that they couldn't handle the situation. A federal task force, commissioned to investigate the problem, had concluded that there was no solution, that nothing could be done.

CIA Director George Bush allegedly worked to convince the former OPMONGOOSE operators to reorganize outside the United States. In June 1976, they went to the Dominican Republic and founded CORU, a counter-revolutionary group. On October 26, 1976, they blew up an airplane that was taking off from Barbados, killing 73 passengers on board in a raw act of terrorism. Luis Posada Carrilles and Orlando Bosch were jailed in Venezuela for that bombing. There is evidence that members of this same CIA/Cuban exile community participated in the killing of President John F. Kennedy in 1963. We also know that the CIA's 1980 *contra* program later managed to get Luis Posada Carrilles out of prison in Venezuela. They put him to work for Felix Rodriguez, who was reporting directly to then Vice-President Bush's Office. As Felix Rodriguez told the press, "We needed him." He was referring to Carrilles, the terrorist airplane bomber.

The Iran/*contra* scandal revealed the very curious situation in which Vice-President George Bush, supposedly in charge of the country's top anti-drug task force, was involved with the drug-running *contras.* In the early 1980s, Bush travelled to Panama to meet with Noriega, who was then cooperating with the "Black Eagle" operation that supplied arms to the *contras* and was using Panamanian airstrips. In the mid-1980s, the CIA had a falling out with Noriega, apparently because he refused to cooperate with its plans for the invasion of Nicaragua. The *contra* resupply operation was then shifted to the Ilopango airbase in El Salvador, and Felix Rodriguez was put in charge. (Testimony and evidence presented in the Milian Rodriguez trial and to the Kerry Committee showed that the Medellin cocaine cartel was making payments through Felix Rodriguez, buying access to the *contra* air transport program that was being run out of Ilopango.) Hard evidence, international telephone records for example, proves that Rodriguez was reporting several times a week to Vice-President Bush's office.

Another example is when the Hasenfus plane crashed in Nicaragua in 1986 and Bush's office was the first to be informed. On several previous occasions, Rodriguez had flown up to Washington to report to the Vice-President, and on three occasions he met with Bush himself.

Bush says he does not remember ever talking to Rodriguez and Donald Gregg (his liaison with the *contras* during his term as Vice-President) about the *contra* program or activities down in Central America. They just chatted about their lunch or dinner or something. This is not very plausible. With Ronald Reagan, you could believe that he didn't understand when people briefed him—the man's mind skipped in and out, as everyone well knew. But George Bush is intelligent. It is very difficult to believe that he would not be aware of these things. Even if they did talk only about lunch, when the drugs and terrorist connections became public information, even perfunctorily investigated by the Congress, Bush did not purge himself of these associations. You see, he *couldn't,* because of the dirty history of his involvement with such men. Instead, when he became President, he nominated Donald Gregg to be Ambassador to South Korea.

All of this is very public information. Is it any wonder that, during the winter of 1987, *conservative columnists* were writing in the major media that Bush's political career was dead, that he could never survive the Iran/*contra* scandal? I wasn't so sure, but thought that if he did not win the power and protection of the presidency, he stood a very good chance of going to jail. To the columnists' apparent astonishment, Bush plowed ahead. They should not have been surprised.

Looking at George Bush's policies after almost two years in office, one can begin to measure the personality of his presidency. He is more subtle than Ronald Reagan, and less noisy, but he is continuing Reagan's policies across the globe. Bush refused the Soviets' offer for both superpowers to abstain from delivering arms to the combatants in Afghanistan; he continued to deliver arms to Jonas Savimbi in Angola—including Stinger ground-to-air missiles—after Savimbi has boasted openly of shooting down passenger planes; he asked for military aid for the *contras* in Nicaragua so they could continue fighting; and he pressed ahead with vigorous plans to interfere with the elections in Nicaragua. The latter was an eventual success for George Bush and the CIA.

George Bush has continued military support for the death squads in El Salvador and, under the guise of the War on Drugs, he is putting the U.S. military into other Latin American countries—Peru, for example—where they are doing the same thing that they have been doing in El Salvador: flying planes, strafing and rocketing villages.

To demonstrate his decisiveness, he ordered the invasion of Panama in December 1989 and in August 1990 plunged U.S. forces into the Middle East in response to the Iraqi invasion of Kuwait. In the recent crisis, the Saudi Arabian oil that seems to be at stake is not even a primary source of the United States' energy supply. It is exported mainly to Germany and Japan. In this crisis, the United States is functioning as the "Praetorian Guard" of the world financial powers. Although the United States is laboring under a gigantic debt, and Germany and Japan are the undisputed economic winners of the Cold War, the U.S.—still a gigantic military power—has plunged in to police Iraq and protect the wealthier countries' oil. And we are footing a lion's share of the bill.

There is another reason behind Bush's popular, decisive response in the Middle East. He, and the U.S. interests he represents, urgently need a war. As former CIA Director, as former Vice-President, and as the father of Neil Bush who was part of the Silverado S & L scandal, Bush is deeply involved in the Savings and Loan crisis. He stands in line to receive the blame for the economic mess that currently threatens U.S. economic power after a decade of massive over-spending.

I predicted the U.S. invasion of Panama in the spring of 1989 based on an estimate of President Bush's need for a military adventure and on the visible orchestration of public opinion against Manuel Noriega. In the winter of 1990, there was a similarly visible orchestration of public opinion against Cuba, held to be the "last redoubt of Stalinism in the post Cold War world." The *Miami Herald* ran articles about how Cuban exiles were selling their banks and businesses in order to have liquid capital to gain a running start in the new Cuba, after Fidel's overthrow. Bumper stickers read "Home Before Xmas." Meetings were hosted by the likes of Theodore Shackley, who once directed the CIA's JMWAVE station on the University of Miami campus from which the CIA's OPMONGOOSE secret war against Cuba was directed in the early 1960s. And the Television Marti balloon was launched to beam propaganda into Cuba in an obvious attempt to provoke Castro into reactions and mistakes.

I believed that the orchestration against Cuba would continue and eventually, perhaps in 1992, justify a blunt military confrontation. Something on the order of Grenada or Panama would not do because of the size of the economic problems and scandals the Bush administration was facing. Something closer to the challenge of Vietnam was needed, but of course they wanted a defeatable challenger. Cuba seemed to fit; it would be a tough opponent, and the losses would be substantial, but the island could be submitted to a total naval blockade and crushed within a few months by an all-out U.S. effort.

Iraqi President Saddam Hussein gave President Bush an early Christmas present and let Cuba off the hook, at least temporarily. With the Iraqi invasion and conquest of Kuwait, Bush was handed his much-needed war on a silver platter. Hussein, columnists have noted, was surprised by Bush's all-out reaction. But the U.S. war fever was predictable. At this point, even an all-out war would be in Bush's political interests, presuming the United States could win.

Time, however, was on Hussein's side. Bush's decisive reaction has been enormously popular in the United States, but the economic price would be felt soon enough. The United States cannot afford a $25 million per day military adventure in the Middle East, not to mention the billion-dollar-a-day cost of an all-out war, according to estimates from the Center for Defense Information.

Like the Reagan/Bush military extravagance of the 1980s, these bills will come due. Bush will be held responsible for the costs of his Middle East adventure, but Cuba is still there, an enemy in our own backyard, on the back burner for now, but a good possibility as the next distraction.

For some it will be shocking, even offensive, that I suggest Bush and others of our nation's leaders systematically lie and lead us into war, but if they will reflect a moment it will seem less so. Everyone knows that politicians routinely exaggerate, distort, and make promises that they know full well they can never fulfill. They are selling illusions of themselves; they are coached and packaged by professional public relations teams who have made a science out of the marketing of politics. War, too, is packaged and sold. Woodrow Wilson campaigned in 1912 promising to keep the United States out of World War I. Franklin Delano Roosevelt campaigned in 1940, very careful not to appear as if he wanted to take the nation into World War II on the side of the British. Lyndon Johnson promised in 1964 that Americans boys would not die in Vietnam. Once elected, each of those presidents did lead the nation into wars in which hundreds of thousands of young American soldiers died. Moreover, most of the dead, without understanding the issues, had been conditioned to believe that it was proper for them to fight and die.

At the presidential level, highly professional staffs orchestrate public opinion to support their agenda, while carefully watching the polls. For example, *Washington Post* columnists Rowland Evans and Robert Novak reported that before the bombing of Libya on April 12, 1986, White House pollsters had secretly polled the nation until they were certain the people had accepted President Reagan's and Secretary of State George Shultz's depiction of Libya's Muammar Quadafi as the source of the international terrorism that they said was the scourge of the modern world. The bombing was a political coup. The nation was thrilled.

Coincidentally, that bombing also distracted the nation from the fact that President Reagan was to leave a few days later for an economic summit meeting of Western world leaders in Tokyo in which the bad news would become public that the United States had become a debtor nation for the first time since before World War I. At the summit, Reagan successfully prevailed upon other leaders and the media to focus on terrorism, a much more exciting subject than debts and unsolvable trade deficits.

People individually and collectively are manipulable creatures. Marine Corps boot camp taught me that. They conditioned us into a mental state where we were mindless, screaming, potential killers, all fired up and ready to "Charge!" up whatever hill without asking why—and ignoring the fact that we might well not come back down on our own feet. If you do not defend yourself by filling your mind with a true understanding of what is happening in the world, then others will fill it for you; and at some point in time use the information and the conditioning that they have done on your mind, the ideas and feelings they have planted in your breast, to manipulate you to their purpose.

The orchestration of public concern about terrorism was so successful before the bombing of Libya in 1986 that thousands of Americans canceled travel to Europe out of fear that they would be kidnapped or machine-gunned in some airport. The ultra-macho Chicago Bears football team canceled plans to visit Europe, with their spokesman, the quarterback Jim McMahon expressing his fear of terrorism. The Europeans couldn't understand what our concern was about. In fact, Secretary Shultz gave the program away when he said that 78 Americans had been killed in terrorist acts in the 18 months before the bombing; the *New York Times* published a report that put the figure at 28 in the preceding 12 months. This would place terrorism somewhere between rattlesnake bites and choking to death on gristle in restaurants as a threat to our longevity, and light years behind the *real* threats: the 50,000 automobile accidents we tolerate each year, the 450 Americans who are murdered each week, and the more than a million who die of tobacco- and diet-related diseases annually.[4]

We *want* to believe our leaders; we accept politicians' summaries of our interests, thoughts and reactions with mindless faith, even while we all know the rules of the games they play. We are equally ambivalent about the CIA. Every American knows that the agency runs operations out there in the "alleys and gutters of the world" that are improper, illegal, and sometimes depraved. Yet most of us feel that somehow we *need* this activity, even when it measurably damages our national security. For example, Lt. Col. Oliver North is one of the ten best-liked men in the United States as a result of having done far more damage to his commander-in-chief Ronald Reagan's presidency than all the Democrats and detractors combined.

While North boasted that he would take the spears in his chest and stand on his head for the commander-in-chief, he hid behind the Fifth Amendment. He wore his uniform and medals while lying to the Congress under oath. He shredded his files, desperate to destroy evidence of activities that would lead to possible imprisonment and the impeachment of his President. His management of covert operations from the White House was erratic and unprofessional; files that he was not able to burn reveal that he knew drugs were being smuggled through the Nicaraguan *contra* activities he orchestrated.

The 1980s was not a great decade for the Marines.[5] While Oliver North was desecrating the uniform he claimed to wear with such pride, Sgt. Longtree was getting himself seduced by KGB agents in Moscow. Bud MacFarlane, who was a lieutenant in my own Basic School class in Quantico, Virginia in 1959, was Oliver North's boss in the National Security Council. You recall, during the scandal, he attempted suicide by taking Valium. (Gordon Liddy, a civilian, would have used a .357 magnum, and he wouldn't have missed!) During the Iran/*contra* hearings, Oliver North somberly reported that when he and MacFarlane had flown to Iran on CIA Director William Casey's orders, they had taken a "substance" along, in case they were captured. In testimony before another committee he admitted that the substances they had taken was not an esoteric "L-pill." It was Valium! Picture the scene in Iran had they been taken prisoner and were facing torture: "Wait!" they insist to their captors, "We've got to take our Valium!"

It is not my intention to pillory Lt. Col. North, George Bush, or any other individual. They illustrate an American syndrome that is a factor in our traditional enthusiasm for wars. While North is a seasoned combat veteran, he also deceives and shamelessly plays to his audience through the same television and film medium that brings us our war hero/actors. Ronald Reagan often boasted that he had seen four wars, while in fact he had seen them from the safe but exciting Hollywood battlefield stage sets where the blood was catsup, and after a good combat scene of goose-bump-raising valor and tragic heroism there awaited a hot shower and glamourous parties.

More recently, the actor Tom Selleck portrayed an appealing Vietnam veteran in his "Magnum P.I." series, and, although Hawaii was the closest he ever came to combat in Vietnam, he became caught up in the heroism of his television role and today uses his fame to sell macho, conservative values. Sylvester Stallone, whose depiction of a troubled combat veteran in *Rambo* became the modern prototype of the deadly hero, spent the Vietnam War working on the staff of a rich-girls' school in Switzerland, pleading physical disability for further insulation against the draft. Gordon Liddy, yesteryear's spokesman for the far right, exhorts young people to stand up and fight Communism, although he did not fight Communists when he was of an age to do so. Instead, he ran sloppy, unprofessional breaking-and-entering operations that eventually brought down his President, Richard Nixon, in the Watergate scandal.

My own hands are far from clean, although unlike Reagan, Selleck, Stallone, Liddy, and even John Wayne, I did join the Marines and I was awarded a high CIA medal for my conduct in Vietnam at the end of the war. I ran bugging operations with the highest professional standards. In Angola in the 1970s, we broke many of the same laws that North broke in the 1980s, except there was no drug smuggling in that part of Africa, nor did we divert arms to deadly enemies who were taking Americans hostage. And, after the experience, I have obviously grown in a very different direction than my former colleagues.

MY STORY

I have been called a traitor for speaking out against the crimes of the CIA, and threats have been made against my life on national television. On the other hand, many thousands of people have written expressing their appreciation, and supporting me in many other ways. Often they inquire about the process that made me, and others like me, change so profoundly. In fact, I changed less than people realize when I left the CIA and became its critic. I am the same moral and ethical person that I was as a young Marine captain or a CIA operative. It is my understanding of the world and of that infrastructure that I was part of that changed so dramatically. I had been reared and trained to believe I was doing the right thing, that I was serving the highest interests of humankind, in the Marine Corps and the CIA. I am a historical conservative, spelled with a small c, not to be confused with right-wing Conservatives like Senator Jesse Helms or radicals like ex-President Ronald Reagan, who proposed disregarding the Constitution and dropping "demonstration" nuclear weapons in Europe.

My background is conservative. My paternal grandfather was a lawyer in east Texas; my great-grandfather was a doctor. My other grandfather built houses in the Houston area. My father worked for Dow Chemical Company. My earliest memories are steeped with World War II propaganda and patriotism. I remember hiding behind pine trees in our yard in Louisiana when I was four, watching General George Patton's tanks rumbling by, training for the invasion of Africa; fascinated by the fighter aircraft that were parked in the town square for us to ogle after watching the news briefs that were appended to every movie we watched; watching my uncles coming home on furlough in their uniforms and carving little rifles for me while I sat in their laps and they told me about their adventures.

Obviously I was not educated to the harsh realities and cynicism of war. The Americans were always the Good Guys. I didn't even realize that the Russians had played a role (much less the greater role) in defeating Hitler. Equally obvious, this

31

childhood conditioning affected decisions and mistakes I would make for the rest of my life.

Immediately after the war, when he was released from the defense plant, my father answered a Presbyterian Church ad for an engineer who would move to the Belgian Congo to build a hydroelectric plant for a mission hospital. My mother managed a small orphan's home and the only modern women's academy in Central Africa. I became bi-lingual and bi-cultural. My playmates were Congolese boys. We roamed and hunted the grassy plains and the rain forests along the river bottoms. I learned how to drive in a 5-ton truck. Missionaries, including doctors, preachers, and teachers, tend to be a well-educated lot with graduate degrees, and, without other distractions, they traditionally took trunkloads of books on their four-year assignments. I was exposed to remarkable libraries and read endlessly when I wasn't hiking, hunting, swimming, canoeing, or building tree houses in forest giants. It was an unusually rich and exciting childhood.

I attended the University of Texas during one of the most conservative eras in U.S. history—the 1950s. While Senator Joseph McCarthy was witch-hunting Communists in Washington, I was volunteering for the ROTC. We got our hair cut once a week, shined our shoes every morning, and said "sir" to all adult men and "ma'am" to all women.

At the University of Texas, I got into the elite Plan II special reading program and obtained a Naval ROTC scholarship, graduating with what the university billed as its best possible liberal arts degree. Then I took the Marine Corps option and made my way into the elite parachute-and-UDT trained 2nd Force Reconnaissance Company. Only years later did I realize that I had obtained the best *half*-education available. They taught me the classics; we studied philosophy and history with award-winning professors (including John Silber of Boston University). But my generation didn't question. We scribbled furiously in our notebooks, trying to capture the professor's exact words so we could regurgitate them faithfully back to him (there were no women professors in my program at that time) in the examinations. Throughout my school years, I never had a conversation with a liberal, much less a radical critic of the system, or even a serious questioner. There was one professor, Clarence Ayers, who occasionally made a suggestive comment, but he was under constant pressure from the Texas legislature, not to mention the university's regents.

There were indications that I wasn't brain-dead. I published an article in the student newspaper entitled "From the Atheist," and was dropped from consideration as a potential member of the Pershing Rifles fraternity. The ROTC major called me in and expressed concern about my judgment. I also clipped a political cartoon in which ant creatures are rushing up a hill to plunge over a cliff into the sea. One is sitting on a rock, thinking about it. The others are calling, "Hurry up or you'll be left behind."

I was able to get into the 2nd Force Reconnaissance company because events were heating up in the Congo (now Zaire), where I had grown up, and I was one of the very few Americans who spoke the languages. My three years of service were between wars and gloriously, wonderfully fun, playing with parachutes and airplanes, locking out of submarines in the azure waters near St. Thomas, sort of like post-adolescent Boy Scouts but with real toys. There was only one moment, when we were standing by on a ship off the mouth of the Congo River with our weapons loaded, preparing to land, when I had serious doubts. The thought occurred to me that in a few minutes I might be shooting Congolese, possibly including some of my childhood buddies. I didn't like the thought and I'm not sure what I would have done, but the landing was scrubbed and I did not have to make the decision.

After my three years were up, I got out of the Marine Corps. It was a scary decision, because I didn't know what I would do, and I liked the Corps. I liked the security of it all. But I had two small children and the Corps was preparing to send me to Okinawa and then on sea duty, possibly away from my family for four years. That didn't seem to be the responsible thing for me to do as a father. I worked for two years in a ranching and land-clearing business in south Texas, then in the sales and market analysis branch of the Gates Rubber Company in Denver for a couple of years.

I was a captain in the reserves, still gung-ho, and still missing the Marines. I was restless. It was 1963 and Jack Kennedy was President. He had challenged us to "Ask not what your country can do for you, but what you can do for your country." With Bobby Kennedy, his brother, he put together "Camelot" in Washington with the "best and the brightest" of our society.

They were also putting out a good deal of anti-Communist propaganda. This was the height of the "domino theory," and I was very responsive because that was exactly what they had taught us in the Marine Corps. None of us understood the broader workings of society. We weren't skeptical. The Vietnam War and Watergate and the investigations of the mid-1970s—of the Church Committee, for example—had not yet happened. Nor had the sexual, feminist, civil rights, and drug revolutions happened. We especially didn't know anything about the CIA. We didn't know that the CIA was paying professors to publish 1,200 propagandistic books about places like the Soviet Union, Vietnam, China, Cuba, and the Congo, or that they were experimenting on U.S. citizens with drugs.

I didn't *question* anything about life. When we heard the announcement at the office that President Kennedy had been shot, my boss whooped with delight and said, "Thank God somebody finally shot the bastard." But by the next day we "knew" it had been the work of a lone, loony assassin. Not one person I knew suspected there might be a conspiracy, much less one that involved branches of the government.

In the 1964 elections, I voted for Barry Goldwater (who was running against Lyndon Johnson), the Republican arch-Conservative. This was in part because everyone in Texas knew that Lyndon Johnson was corrupt to the core, with mob ties, with murders sometimes associated with his political campaigns. It was also in part because of Goldwater's attitude toward Vietnam, namely that we would go in and *win,* using atomic weapons if we had to. I reasoned that I wasn't wise enough to judge whether or not we should be involved in Vietnam, but if we were, Goldwater's proposed policy made sense to me: Win.

The CIA first contacted me by letter in 1964, using Central

Intelligence Agency stationery. They quietly asked for permission to do a background check with the objective of offering me employment. Obviously they check a lot of people's backgrounds without advising them. The purpose was to get me to thinking of a CIA career while they did the background check. Besides, I was a good risk. A gung-ho Marine. And I still had my security clearance.

Waiting for them to complete their check, I tried to prepare myself. Despite my childhood in Africa, I felt painfully ignorant of diplomacy and covert activities. I set out to read whatever books I could find on the subject, and inadvertently hit on one of the CIA's propaganda books. It was a biography of Karl Marx that presented him as a long-haired radical, who lived in a squalid garret in London without ever bathing, beating his wife, spawning illegitimate children, and propounding mad theories about world revolution. The book impressed me so much that when I got into CIA training where we studied Communism— the enemy—seriously for a year, I found myself arguing with the professors. But Karl Marx was a nut, I would protest, and they would laugh and assure me that he had developed theories that had influenced the thinking of more than half the world's population.

In retrospect, it seems clear that I was a latent questioner, a potential questioner, and one may wonder why the CIA testing, which is perhaps the most comprehensive in the world, didn't screen me out. They put me through many days of every kind of test imaginable, from IQ to personality to aptitude. Written and oral. I was wise about tests and did everything I could to make myself look good in them so the CIA would hire me. In the first one, a Mickey Mouse IQ test administered for the CIA by a graduate student from the University of Denver, the guy set me to working and then talked and joked loudly over the phone while I worked. I thought it might be part of the test, and did not protest. Later I realized it wasn't—the guy was a jerk.

The other tests were easy enough to finesse. I brainstormed the kind of profile that I thought the CIA would like, i.e., aggressive, thoughtful but also restrained. In the dozens of five-part multiple choice selections I would always mark one of the middle three, avoiding the "I *strongly* dislike (or *strongly* like)..." answers. When they asked if I preferred to watch basketball or to play tennis, I chose tennis—they would surely want someone active. Listen to music or go shopping—I went shopping. If I was driving past the scene of an accident and observed that the drivers were coming to blows, I drove on past. (In a Marine Corps test I would have stopped and tried to calm them down.)

They told us that the security people had checked every detail of our lives, all the way back to our childhoods. Every school we had attended, every teacher, the neighbors at every place we had lived, every problem we had ever had. I believed them and was impressed, at first. On the lie detector, they asked all the "obvious" questions about drugs, homosexuality, and Communist Party affiliation. And about the KKK. When they asked me about the Communist Party, I passed without a blip. Their research had not turned up the "Big Boy's Communist Party" in my boarding school past. Being a little boy at the time, I was only an honorary member of the BBCP. None of us, of course, had the foggiest idea of what Communism was, and none of us had ever heard of Karl Marx, but we vaguely (and inappropriately) associated the Communist Party with secret rebellion against authority, which we found appealing. The much-ballyhooed security check hadn't turned up our little adventure. I wondered if they would have hired me if they had. I also wondered about the efficacy of the lie detector test.

Some parts of the tests were done with psychologists watching. For example, they would put three of us in a room and give us problems, blocks of wood to play with, to solve jointly, while they observed. I blew this test, because I thought they were comparing us and measuring our relative smarts. Hence I sat back quietly, studied the problem, and then offered solution after solution. It turned out that they were looking for indicators of how we tended to work together with other people, and to my horror the psychologists recommended that I be put in the overt, analytical side of the CIA. I wanted to be in operations, and I had to labor for weeks to look more like an operator than an analyst.

At the end of all the testing, the psychologists called me in for a conference and told me that I was smart and competent, above average, but that I was most effective when I played things straight, when I did not try to be imaginative, clever, or funny. After I got to know my classmates in training better, I found, significantly, that they had each been told the same thing.

In one of the interviews, the training officer pressed me about my background on the Presbyterian mission in the Congo. He was concerned that I might not have the moral fortitude to do the job. Of course, he would not say what job, but eventually he pushed me so hard that I stood to walk out. "Look," I told him. "I was a captain in Marine Corps recon. But if you're looking for someone to stick knives in people's backs and to slit throats, literally," I said, "I'm in the wrong place. I couldn't do that." He hastened to sit me back down. (He would have gotten a bad mark on his fitness report if he had let me walk out that door.) With my Marine recon training and my experience, languages, and knowledge of the Congo, I was a model recruit.

I was, in fact, so strong a candidate that I could easily have bargained, I soon learned, for a GS 10, step 5, instead of accepting the GS 9 they offered me. I presumed that it was like the Marine Corps, where everyone starts as a second lieutenant, and never asked. A Good Soldier! When I met some of my colleagues, one of whom had bargained a mediocre background into a higher grade, I still didn't complain. That probably made me a dream recruit.

In training they worked hard to reassure us that we were the Good Guys of the intelligence business. For one thing, there was no goon talk. It was all very high-minded. In the world's richest spy school, for example, the word "spy" was never used. It has a pejorative ring. We were not seducing people to commit treason against their own countries. We were inviting them to join us in the desperate, secret struggle to save the world. In our training exercises, we were encouraged to take care of our "agents," to make them feel like better people for working with us. There was not a single class on blackmail, or even "control" of an agent through coercion. Positive motivation was emphasized. The course was literally structured from and grounded in

Dale Carnegie's principles of *How To Win Friends And Influence People.*

I loved it. In one of the exercises we went out into town to meet instructors who were posing as potential agents. I noticed that mine was limping, asked about it, and was told he had the gout. I suggested that he might not be receiving the best medicine available, which I might be able to obtain from the United States (this exercise was supposedly happening in Egypt). Back at the training facility (Camp Peary, Virginia) I checked with the medics, explaining the problem, and in the spirit of the thing they gave me some pills to pass to him in our next meeting. He was delighted, accepted my recruitment, and I got an "Outstanding" mark for the exercise.

They taught us how to spot, assess, and recruit potential agents. Unlike our KGB counterparts, we were not taught ideology as such; there were no classes on what the United States stood for. Instead we were taught to single out people who had access to some office or service that interested us, to assess their personal interests, what they responded to, what made them tick, and then we were taught to devise approaches to them through their personal interests. If they were venal, we were taught to hint at money; if they were carnal, to tell dirty jokes and maybe go to topless bars for our meetings; if they were religious, to clean up our act. They actually used the chauvinistic analogy of a man trying to seduce a married woman, with her husband representing the security threat. If she played tennis, we would take up tennis and begin meeting her at the courts, chatting casually, always careful to follow her lead and never to be threatening. We had classes titled "Building Rapport." Ideally she would eventually be willing to go bed with us, without our having to ask. It would seem the natural thing to do.

The training was realistic. Later, in the field, I actually witnessed a case where a colleague hurried to take the *Hustler* magazines off his coffee table from one meeting and to put on some classical music and set out copies of the *Catholic Review* for a meeting with another very different developmental contact.

In another case, many years later, I watched a case officer in Managua trying to recruit a woman who had worked for years in the anti-CIA, progressive movement. She had at times risked jail to challenge the CIA. She was in Nicaragua working on a film and met a nice man from the U.S. Embassy. He told her that he personally admired the Sandinistas and what they were trying to do, and struggled in his reporting to provide some balance against all the people in Washington who hated them. The problem was that everyone in Nicaragua mistrusted him. How could he help, how could he get meaningful reports if no one would talk to him? She could help the Sandinistas enormously by meeting with him every now and then, telling him who was who, maybe introducing him to some of the people she knew.

As we recruited people, we had to fill out questionnaires that included biographic information and descriptions. One of the questions was, "Why does this person *want* to work for U.S. intelligence?" The instructors urged us always to put down "For money" assuring us that we would never encounter a problem with headquarters if we did. But in the field I learned it wasn't money. Frequently, the agents didn't really need money. Or they would take the payment and slip it in their pocket uncounted while they were still talking about the operation. Eventually I decided that the predominant motivation was the Walter Mitty factor—the need for a secret fantasy life that would make them special and distinguish them from other people. They wouldn't be just another businessman or professor or government official. They would also have a secret CIA life that they could rationalize in terms of all kinds of special meanings to suit their personal needs. I saw this motivation at work with several chiefs of state in different countries, where they would have me brought up their back stairs in the dark of night, obviously relishing the secret relationship. We also saw it work in the famous case of Oleg Penkovskiy, the KGB general who wanted something more, and eventually paid the ultimate price for his effort.

With all the goodness we were taught, I nevertheless found that, even in training, I sold out an agent's life for ulterior purposes. In the graduation exercise we were sent up to New

York City, where a dummy CIA station was set up by the chief of training in a hotel room. In this scenario, New England was a separate neutral country, and the Midwest a major Communist industrial nation. New York was a free city, like Hong Kong or Paris. We would have contact with an individual who had a family inside the Midwest and traveled back and forth. Because there weren't enough instructors to go around, they had to break us into teams. In the final meeting in another hotel room, we had been instructed to recruit the man to return to Ohio and send out reports about the nuclear weapons plants there. He was being difficult, practical, scared. It couldn't be done. He would be killed. He wasn't a fool. He was so persuasive that one of the members of my team began to agree with him. It wasn't a good idea. We couldn't ask him to risk his life. The instructor began to eye the door, with a malicious glint in his eye.

I stood up and began to pace the floor. The instructors could not have intended for us to fail to make the recruitment, not in the graduation exercise of our positive-minded course. If we let him get out that door and go back to report that we had agreed that he should not work for the CIA, we would be the laughing stock of the class. It was the sort of thing that would transcend training, that people would joke about ten years later. But how to turn him around and get him to accept the recruitment? Hold on, I said. If you say it's that dangerous, I'll take your word for it, although it may be that it seems more dangerous than it is because the idea is new to you. I can imagine it's pretty intimidating. But even if it is life-threatening, you still have to think about it, for your children's sakes, and for all the other children in the world. If nobody is willing to take a chance, we obviously can't stop Communism, and we'll never turn the world around. The end of that road is nuclear war. And if the worst happens, I can guarantee that your children will be cared for all their lives (of course I had no power to make any such guarantee). And besides, you may not realize that we have resources you never dreamed of. There are all kinds of things we can do inside to back you up. (This was off the top of my head, of course, I knew of no capability to do any such thing.) The man began to nod his head, and I talked on. He accepted the recruitment and, for encouraging the individual to risk his life in my professional interests, I got an Outstanding for the exercise and graduated at the top of my class.

In my first actual assignment, I got a young man sentenced to death—literally this time—doing my job and hustling my career. I was responsible for covering a number of countries in West Africa and needed a utility agent who could be my eyes and ears. I found a young man who was related to everyone in power in the country, although his own father was dead and he didn't have his own Mercedes to drive. I gave him money and a secret identity, and he was delighted to work for me. It was my first real recruitment, and the bond between us was very strong. Unfortunately there were no intelligence targets in that country, and after six months headquarters came back with the evaluation that we would have to terminate the operation if the reporting didn't start reflecting something important.

I became a little desperate to save my operation and had meetings with my friend, trying to figure out what we could report that would interest headquarters. There was no Communist presence. Or subversion. Or strategic interests. "What about your cousin," I asked, "the one who was the son of the ousted president? Might he be plotting anything? He can't be very happy, having grown up in the palace and then winding up in poverty." My friend said he didn't see that cousin very often and I berated him. "That is exactly the sort of contact we need to keep our eyes on." I left and returned a couple of weeks later, and he reported that his cousin was in fact restless. The next time I came back his cousin was plotting. Soon enough I was getting recognition from headquarters. They had not thought there was any unrest in this country and I had not only uncovered a coup plot, but had an agent in its inner circles.

As the plot developed, I became increasingly concerned. The plotters were irresponsible youths, whereas the incumbent government was mature, stable, and pro-U.S. Surely we had some responsibility to warn someone. Headquarters was adamant. Our "Country Directive" for that country required us to report events, but not to undertake action. The night before the plot was to strike, the President, who had it penetrated as well, arrested all the plotters, including my friend, and sentenced them to death.

At almost exactly the same time I was promoted and transferred to the position of chief of base in Lubumbashi, in the troubled Katanga province of my old home, the Congo, now Zaire. I flew away, wondering about my friend and steeling myself against my guilt. Would he have been under a death sentence if I had never visited the country? No. Would there even have been a plot if I had not sent him back repeatedly to question his cousin? Quite possibly they had gotten their heads together and hatched the plot in order to please me, thinking that was what I wanted. But my conscience was given a reprieve; the President was a gentle person who commuted their sentences to seven years in prison, then released them after one year, only expelling them from the country.

In Katanga, I dealt with mutinying CIA mercenaries, Jean Schramme and Bob Denard, who were tearing the country apart. They would not have been there doing their violent thing if the CIA had not recruited, funded, armed, and placed them there. I led the convoy of U.S. consular personnel as they were taken across the border into Zambia—my family back in the States caught me on international television at the border—and then returned to sweat out the fighting in my post.

In my next assignment I accidentally got a long-time CIA agent killed. He was a beautiful man who looked like Flip Wilson and was almost as funny to be around. There was no trial. They just picked him up one day and shot him. He had worked for several predecessors and everyone in town knew he was the CIA's friend. In the damage assessment, I went through his thick files and couldn't find a single report he had ever given us that was not duplicated by information overtly obtained without risk by the ambassador and other embassy officers. For no apparent gain on anyone's part, he was dead and his six children were fatherless. As chief of station, my budget for entertaining people was ten times the size of the ambassador and his staff's combined. We were known to be CIA, known to be bribing and corrupting people. To note the obvious, this activity is illegal. At best, it engenders mistrust and ill will.

At a chiefs-of-station conference in Addis Ababa, I drank through the night with Larry Devlin, the notorious officer who had worked to engineer the killing of Patrice Lumumba in the Congo and then went on to manage the CIA's secret war in Laos. He was returning to take charge of Africa Division, and crossing the continent to meet his station chiefs. I told him I didn't think our presence was justified. In six years, in all the countries I had visited, none of the CIA's operations had visibly advanced U.S. national security interests. They had caused problems for the United States by damaging its credibility. He put me down with the same line that numerous presidents have used to reassure the nation: "If you knew the secret information that I know about the world, you would understand why these things are necessary." Devlin told me that there were grey-beards back in Washington who sat in the inner sancta with all the secret knowledge of the world, who were qualified to judge such things. *They* knew that my presence in Burundi was justified, that our presence throughout Africa was justified. I had been overseas too long. I was getting out of touch and too big for my britches. In time I would sit in those inner councils myself. Meanwhile I should get back to my post and get back to work and quit thinking, until he could get me reassigned to his staff back at Langley.

Aye aye, sir! Got a little out of line, sir! It won't happen again, sir! I poured him onto his plane at dawn and returned to Bujumbura thinking that someone ought to write a book that would present the truth about the spy business.

Back in Washington I found that the Department of State very much agreed with my assessment of the CIA's role in Africa. The semi-secret Macomber Report concluded that there was no justification for the CIA's presence throughout Africa. Word went out through the ranks that our Africa Division would be closed down, and I found myself disbelieving that they would fire me. Surely I would be retrained, perhaps for duty against the KGB in the real spy world. Of course, the CIA managed to bend with the blow, to survive, and actually to expand its presence in Africa. Its managers agreed that we had been bogged down in competing with embassies for local political information. We should instead be freed of any such requirements and focus on the hard targets, the Soviets, Chinese, North Koreans, and Middle Europeans. I applauded loudly, for I knew that in small African capitals you could get contact with diplomats and agents from these countries in a way you rarely could in Europe. There might be 600 KGB officers in Rome, but try finding them on a regular basis in that city. In a tiny African capital there was one set of cocktail parties, one swimming pool. There might only be two KGB officers, but you saw them several times a week without even trying.

We were retrained to focus on recruiting agents against the hard targets and very soon we began to get favorable results: five recruits one year, the CIA's managers announced, eight, thirteen. I was excited, and believed these reports, until a good friend went into training for assignment to Moscow. Gleefully he told me one night that he had finally gotten the insider's briefing about the real operations the CIA had going in the Soviet Union. He didn't tell me what those operations were—and I didn't ask—but he said that not one of them was from Africa Division's hard target program. He said that what we were recruiting were the clerks and weak officers who had no access to anything important and were such losers they were shunned by their own colleagues. While they responded to overtures of "rapport" from CIA case officers, they did not return to interesting jobs in Moscow and were not the sort of people who made courageous agents anyway. Moreover, too often their colleagues had noticed and reported their contact with the Americans in Africa, and KGB security thoroughly intimidated them when they returned home.

I was made section chief, supporting the CIA's activities in a broad region. One of the big chiefs came back from overseas looking for some women agents to put in bed with hard target officials, literally. The problem was, the CIA had given up on such activities, which are called "sex operations," because when people begin sleeping together they get confused about other purposes.

This chief was a notoriously hard man, and insiders were generally terrified of him. In addition to being short, overweight, booze-ruddy, acne-faced, and red-eyed from smoking cigars and drinking cognac until 3:00 a.m. because he was too mean to sleep, he would sometimes summarily fire people. He used to say, sometimes to women in restaurants, that women didn't like handsome men, they liked ugly little bastards like him, and quite often, to my eternal amazement, they did. At the same time, he was 100 percent professional, always working, and he had something close to a genius for understanding the people who worked for him, and motivating them.

He sat by my desk to lay down his rules and informed me that he was the best case officer in the business. I said, "The second best," and we stared at each other for a while. After that, we became buddies and, whenever we were in the same city, I was permitted to sit up with him drinking until 3:00 a.m., which was by no means an unmixed blessing.

The Washington, DC vice squad told me that there would be 2,000 potential special access agents working the Republican convention in Miami Beach, and so off we went, he a devout Catholic and I a missionary kid. Our story was that he was a big game hunter from his capital and I was his U.S. agent. He was looking for a woman to help in his office. Early on we would tell her that keeping the clients happy was part of the job. When security had vetted her we would tell her the big game was Communist officials.

So we hit the town, playing the roles; he dressed in a safari suit, I in a sports jacket, hunting potential special access agents. At 4:00 a.m., thoroughly drunk, he made his first recruitment, taking the young woman through all three stages of the recruitment as she came and went bringing us drinks—she was the half-nude cocktail waitress in a penthouse nightclub.

The next afternoon she came to the Fontainebleau Hotel lobby as instructed, where all the retired Mafia mamas and papas sit around. I was staked out nearby behind a newspaper, like Archie Goodwin, and my boss had on a dark suit like a *mafioso* or a mini-Nero Wolfe. The young woman was dressed to go to work, in tights, fishnet stockings, lavender makeup, etc. She was bright enough to realize that she shouldn't be in that hotel, looking like that, but incredibly she had swallowed the unlikely story we two drunks had told her the night before.

Spying him, she squealed, ran across the floor, and leaped into his arms, which didn't look right, either. The hotel manager headed for them, and I scrambled over to intercept him. Unable to think of anything brighter, I said, "Don't mess with it, it's CIA." He said get the fuck out of his hotel.

The young woman turned out to be insufficiently intelligent to handle complicated espionage assignments, but I found another who was as good as any case officer in the CIA. She was introduced to me by the White House Secret Service, a brilliant, warm person who was available when governors and visiting chiefs of state came to town, demanding sex. She loved the idea of doing her thing for national security, and working with her, she and I became deeply involved, which was inevitable, stupid, and complicated things immensely. For altogether different reasons of security her operation was scrubbed.

I found yet another, a nurse, whom I sent to the overseas post and whom we succeeded in getting in bed with a target official in a resort. She returned to report that he was an alcoholic, which we already knew, because we had chatted with him at sufficient cocktail parties, that he had halitosis, which we also knew via the same assessment technique, and that he was impotent, which we also knew because we had a camera hidden in the wall of a certain flophouse.

However, he wasn't stupid; he wouldn't see her again, and in the small world of the CIA there is a good deal of gossip amongst case officers and wives. Disenchanted with what she was hearing about my activities in the world of prostitution, my wife soon sued for divorce. I went to Vietnam, where I would witness from the inside the collapse of South Vietnam and be part of the U.S. flight from the country in April 1975.

After my cumulative doubts from the six years in Africa, my divorce, and the tawdry sex operations, I was in a mood to reflect on what I was doing with my life. The Vietnam assignment was a godsend. We received considerable extra financial benefits for serving in Vietnam, and the government would move my wife and children back to the family home in Texas. By 1973, the U.S. armed forces had all departed, and the United

States was cutting back on its presence; "Vietnamization was the word. The CIA, however, was to maintain a full presence for the time being, in order to encourage the Vietnamese. This meant that there were 600 people with perhaps enough work for 60, if not 16. I expected to spend the next 18 months playing tennis, chess, and judo, and sorting out my thoughts. When the tour was over and my personal problems resolved, I would address my doubts about the spy business.

I got a great deal more than I bargained for. A few days after I arrived the officer in charge of a key province committed suicide, creating an emergency situation. I was considered qualified, having been a chief of station and having a solid paramilitary background. Overnight I found myself in Tay Ninh, just 10 miles from COSVN headquarters (the Communist Command Office in South Vietnam), hidden in the Thien Ngon woods. The official ceasefire was a macabre joke, and heavy fighting flared continuously throughout the region. One day shortly after I arrived at the post, there was an ambush on the edge of town and I witnessed 100 bodies laid in rows in a field near my compound. It took the South Vietnamese a couple of days to haul them away, and the stench became oppressive.

Suddenly, after a free ride in the Marine Corps and after Mickey Mouse operations in our embassies in Africa and in Washington, my career had turned deadly serious. Also a few days after I arrived at the post I learned that a Vietnamese police official on whom I would depend greatly was a practicing sadist. He used a CIA safehouse for his gory distraction, taking prisoners who did not have family protection to the place and carving them up through the night while he drank cognac, eventually throwing the remains in the canal at dawn and going home to sleep off his hangover. I reported him to the CIA chief of station and was politely advised that Vietnamese officials' conduct was not our business, that it wasn't our mission to interfere, that we needed the man for other reasons, and that if I didn't have the stomach for the job I could be reassigned elsewhere but at great expense to my career. Certainly I could have quit, but you only get one such judgmental vote in the spy business, and you are either out, or are shelved in some dull corner for the rest of your career. Moreover, I had come to Vietnam to finance a divorce, and to see Asia. This was Asia.

I closed the safehouse and passed the word that I did not approve of such cruel and murderous activities. The result was that my staff and the local officials were careful not to mention their activities to me for the rest of my tour, which permitted a sort of plausible deniability to my conscience. I could rationalize that I had tried to do the right thing, that it wasn't my fault, that maybe he had curtailed his brutality. Perhaps I had saved a life or two by putting a little pressure on him to restrain himself.

At the end, my post was cut off, often surrounded by the enemy, and shelled nearly every day with their big 130 mm canon and 122 mm rockets. I kept the post open because of an especially vital operation that provided us with invaluable information about the enemy's strategic plans and secrets— information that should have been vital as our forces were defeated and the South conquered. I received the CIA's second highest honor, the Medal of Merit, for my effort, but returned it to the CIA when I resigned in 1977.

Instead of relaying to Washington the vital intelligence I was risking my own and my staff's lives to obtain, the chief of station was attempting to suppress it in Saigon. He was passing it to Communist Hungarian colonels on the International Commission for Control and Security (ICCS), who, he knew, were passing it to Hanoi. They had used classic techniques to recruit him to their purposes, telling him that they were sympathetic to the U.S. dilemma and that they would like to persuade Hanoi that it was not in its interests to humiliate the United States by claiming total victory over the South. If he would only give them information to show good faith to the North Vietnamese, surely... He cooperated so fully that he was even showing them the top secret charts that were used to brief visitors from the White House National Security Council, including one that summarized the CIA's most sensitive sources in Vietnam. Some of the information he gave the North Vietnamese, through the Hungarians, included evidence that we had obtained their plan for the final offensive that was to begin with the capture of my post as a stepping stone to the capture of Saigon. The North Vietnamese army was able to attack Ban Muoi Thuot in Military Region II, instead, catching the south by surprise and cutting the country in two. It was only a matter of four weeks and three days thereafter before the entire country fell.

As it fell, CIA case officers abandoned post after post in panicky haste. Afraid that burning or shipping out files would alert their local employees of plans to flee, they left the files in place along with the employees, thereby identifying them in great detail to the Communists. When these officers returned to Saigon, they were not held up in disgrace, for the CIA Director back in Washington had established a policy of disavowing any responsibility for the CIA's Vietnamese employees. Only the Americans and corrupt high Vietnamese officials would be saved. In the great exodus, 147,000 Vietnamese fled from the South, thousands of them in U.S. aircraft and ships, but only about ten percent of the CIA's employees were saved.[6]

I tried to devise imaginative ways to get our people out. I obtained two coastal barges and moored them with water and rice just around the bend of the Dong Nai River from our regional Bien Hoa headquarters. While the predictable crowds collected on the streets, we could bring my boats up to the shielded river site and take everyone out to sea. But my boss in Military Region III stopped me, confiscating my ships and explaining, "John, you have to understand that it isn't our fault these people have the misfortune of being born Vietnamese."

This was at the end of the 10-year war that followed a previous decade of CIA activity in Vietnam. Two million people had been killed. The equivalent of one 500-pound bomb had been dropped on the country for every citizen. Ninety-thousand *tons* of carcinogenic and toxic materials had been dropped on the country, some of which would poison it for decades to come. We were returning to the "World," to continue our lives, while leaving our Vietnamese cohorts behind.

Bye now!

After three months' leave in Texas, during which I was procrastinating in making plans to leave the CIA, I was hastily summoned to Washington and informed that I was the new

commander of the CIA task force that had been formed to mount
an operation in Angola. I would sit on a subcommittee of the
National Security Council, the inner sanctum that Larry Devlin
had promised that I would eventually penetrate five years
before. With many a doubt I took the job. It was irresistible to
me, at whatever price to my soul, for if I refused I would never
know if the activities I had witnessed in the field were in fact as
mindless as they had seemed. I had access to nearly every
document that pertained to the Angolan operation, including
the eyes-only, one-copy-only memos to the President.

In the meetings of the National Security Council, busy,
important men come together to make decisions about U.S.
policy on various problems all over the world. The Secretary of
State, Secretary of Defense, Vice-President, sometimes the President, the CIA Director, people like that, with enormous responsibilities and power. They are aware of their power. The
etiquette is that they do not keep each other waiting. They try
not to show up 30 minutes late to those meetings, because the
other people are powerful and busy too—and they really are
busy. That is one thing I noticed about people in those positions:
they do work hard, long hours, long days, lots of meetings,
keeping a lot of balls in the air.

In the first briefings on the Angola operation, the CIA
Director, William Colby, with an aide with a flip chart, literally
said, "Gentleman, this is a map of Africa. Here is Angola. Now,
there are three factions in Angola. The FNLA (National Front
for the Liberation of Angola), they are the Good Guys; we have
been working with them for fourteen years." And then he
described the FNLA, and Holden Roberto, our rebarbative ally.
Then he said, "The MPLA (Popular Movement for the Liberation
of Angola), they are the Bad Guys, led by the drunken psychotic
poet"—that was what we had written into the briefing material—"Augustino Neto." And he used those words—"Good
Guys" and "Bad Guys"—so these busy men would not be confused about the issues, and proceeded to brief them.

One day Henry Kissinger came to the meeting late, and
everyone had to wait. Now mind you, this is not a meeting of
the Supreme Court, where law prescribes where everybody sits,

according to seniority. The National Security Council, at least at that time, met in an office in the White House, with an oak table and some drapes and some maps, but no electronic flashing boards or anything like that. People sat around the great big table, with the staffers sitting in an outer ring of chairs so they could lean forward to advise their individual masters. Often staffers were not present when sensitive decisions were being made.

The Secretary of Defense plopped down in a chair to talk to somebody while we waited for Kissinger, and then Kissinger came steaming in and he told the Secretary of Defense, "I am here. We can go to work. Move down to your chair." To which the Secretary of Defense replied, "Well, I am all spread out here. You sit there today." And Kissinger said, "No, I am the Secretary of State, this is my chair. You sit down there." They proceeded to argue like five-year-olds for about five minutes. Eventually the Secretary of Defense would not move, and Kissinger had to go sit down at the far end of the table, but he turned his back on the briefings and sulked. He wouldn't pay attention to what we were saying that day because he couldn't have his chair—and we were making decisions that were getting people killed in Angola. I am not exaggerating that incident one bit.

When the operation was formally launched by the National Security Council in January 1975, Angola was moving toward peaceful elections as it gained its independence. The CIA introduced fighting forces into the country, forcing a violent, undemocratic solution instead. (See the Angola section of the next chapter for a summary of the entire fiasco.) The program was stopped by the U.S. Congress in the winter of 1975-76.

I spent six months reviewing the files and then resigned from the agency. After publishing a letter in the *Washington Post* on April 10, 1977, I testified for five days to congressional committees, eschewing the protections of the Fifth Amendment, while I gave them chapter and verse of what we had done in the misguided Angola operation. I gave them the numbers, dates and texts of cables and memoranda that proved we had broken laws and then lied about breaking them. I gave them the combinations to the safes where the documents were stored, and told them where in CIA headquarters those safes could be found. I challenged them to investigate thoroughly and do their duty.

They did nothing. The hearings had been conducted in secret, and after the Watergate scandal, the ouster of President Nixon, and the defeat in Vietnam, they were not willing to tackle another big scandal that might oblige them to put Henry Kissinger and the CIA Director in jail. I proceeded to write my first book, *In Search of Enemies,* to make the public aware of what had happened so they could judge for themselves. It remains today the only insider's account of a major CIA operation.

A year later, when Congress had had abundant time to investigate the secret scandal and prosecute the felons involved, *In Search of Enemies* was published. Without claiming that the book revealed any sensitive secrets, the CIA sued me and succeeded in seizing all future earnings. They also placed me under a court order which requires that all future writings for publication be submitted to the CIA Publications Review Board for censorship.

Since then, I have been on the greatest human adventure imaginable, of growth and of learning all the things about the world that they did not teach us in college. I began to read book after book about the United States and world security problems, and to meet the authors of some of them and talk to them about their findings. I travelled to countries that had been the targets of CIA destabilizations, including Grenada, Jamaica, Cuba, Nicaragua, El Salvador, Honduras, Panama, and Vietnam. In my travels I met people like Carl Sagan, Admiral Gene LaRocque, Admiral Gene Carroll, Jr., Director of the Center for Defense Information, anti-nuclear activist Helen Caldicott, Daniel Ortega, the martyred Grenadan leader Maurice Bishop, and numerous other authorities on national security and the nuclear arms race. I was invited to lecture and have addressed over 600 audiences, learning much from them in return. I have enjoyed the experience more than I could ever have imagined.

Much of this learning process was very personal. In March 1963 I was in Grenada for the anniversary celebration of the New Jewel Movement's takeover. At a cocktail party in a garden overlooking the Caribbean we received the news that President Reagan had given a speech announcing that Grenada was a threat to U.S. national security. The Minister of Education, Jacqueline Creft joked that they had been caught on the eve of their attack on the United States. She said their armies were about to take Washington and New York (Grenada is a small island, about 8 by 16 miles, with 80,000 people, and at the time had two poorly trained and equipped parapolice companies in its armed forces). They would sweep west and capture Chicago by the early summer and then launch their march on California. Everyone laughed, but I pointed out that President Reagan's speech wasn't really funny. If, out of all the million important things he could mention in a public address, he focusses on a country like Grenada and asserts that it is a threat to the "national security" it means that he is drawing attention to it in preparation for attacking it. Creft flared back at me, noting that I didn't need to lecture *them* about U.S. policy. They had been living under the wing and talon of the U.S. eagle for centuries; they knew its dangerous ways too well. But she was glad I was beginning to understand.

As I learned more and more about the history and cynicism of the CIA's so-called secret wars, I also became more concerned about other major problems of world security, including the nuclear arms race, drug smuggling, the abuse of the environment, and the coming world economic crisis. Until we learn to control human behavior at the level of covert destabilizations against countries like Nicaragua, for example, I doubt seriously whether we shall be safe from the planet-threatening aspects of the nuclear arms race.

SECRET THIRD WORLD WARS

I helped to manage three of the CIA's so-called "secret wars" or "low-intensity conflicts":[7] the Congo (now Zaire) in 1967-1969; upcountry in Vietnam in 1973-1975; and I was the chief of the Angola task force in 1975-1976.

After leaving the government in 1977, I made it a point to study these three "secret wars" in depth, as well as many others, and to visit the sites of historic and on-going covert operations. It is impossible to analyze all of these operations in detail in this book, much less the hundreds of others that we have in the public record. Hence I shall select a few in order to illustrate the nature of covert operations. In my choices, I can only appologize to the thousands of slighted victims in El Salvador, Guatemala, the Ukraine, etc.

ANGOLA

The Angola operation is the subject of my book, *In Search of Enemies.* Although Angola is far from the United states geographically and it is certainly far from most Americans' minds, the CIA operation there is a useful case study.

In April 1974, the army rebelled in a coup in Portugal, making it clear that the colony of Angola, where a prolonged independence struggle had been fought, would be granted its freedom. The superpowers quickly chose sides between the three competing factions. The United States automatically sided with the FNLA (Front for the National Liberation of Angola), with whose leader, Holden Roberto, it had maintained contact over the years. In fact, Roberto was close to the Zairian President Mobutu Sese Seku, whom the CIA had installed and maintained in power since 1961. Historically the Soviet Union had generally sided with the MPLA (Popular Movement for the Liberation of Angola), although contact had been disrupted in the years preceding 1974. Reacting to Soviet policy, Communist China sent 400 tons of arms to the FNLA, and over 100 advisors. A

third movement, UNITA (the National Union for the Independence of Angola), was left without a major sponsor. Led by Jonas
Savimbi, it was historically the most radical of the three parties,
having received aid from China, North Korea, South Africa, and
others over the years.

In January 1975, leaders of the three movements met under
Portuguese arbitration and signed the Alvor Accord in which
they agreed to compete peacefully in elections that would be
held in October. November 11 was fixed as the anticipated date
of independence.

Within a week, the National Security Council met in Washington D.C. and allocated $300,000 for the FNLA's use in the
political campaign. The FNLA had sufficient arms from the
Chinese and from Zaire and a record of bloody violence against
the Portuguese and the MPLA. The CIA station chief in Kinshasa
urged Roberto to move his FNLA forces inside Angola. His men
went in armed and soon attacked and killed a team of MPLA
organizers. At that moment the Alvor Accord was effectively
sabotaged and the fate of Angola sealed in blood.

During the spring all of the factions scrambled to organize,
obtain arms, and establish control over whatever territory they
could. The MPLA was by far the most successful. By mid-sum-
mer, it controlled 13 of the 15 provinces. The National Security
Council, which was dominated by Henry Kissinger, demanded
a paper outlining possible options from the CIA. This was July
1975, just three months after the last helicopter had left the
embassy rooftop in Saigon, marking the decisive end of the
Vietnam War. Many, including CIA Director William Colby
were surprised that the CIA would move so quickly into another
adventure.

The CIA's paper offered four options: one for $600,000
which would provide political support for the FNLA; one for $6
million which would include some military support; one for $14
million which would involve substantial military; and one for
$40 million. The $40 million, it was estimated, would equal
anything the Soviet Union was likely to try in Angola. These
options and the estimate of the Soviet reaction were not the
result of a massive study. The CIA's Africa Division chief and

his staff plucked the figures out of a round table discussion, and Colby relayed them to Henry Kissinger as authoritative. It must be noted that neither the Africa Division chief nor his deputy had *any* substantive experience in Africa. One had spent his career in Europe, the other in the Pacific Basin. Only the deputy had any substantive experience in managing paramilitary activity: he had been part of the programs that had just dramatically failed in Southeast Asia, and had never set foot in Africa.

A fifth option, staying out of the conflict and letting Angola make its own way toward independence, was not included in the paper. Was this a viable option? The Assistant Secretary of State for African Affairs, Ambassador Nathaniel Davis, firmly believed so. Of the proposed CIA program, he said, "It's the wrong game for a great nation, and the players we've got are losers." The U.S. Consul General in the Angolan capital of Luanda, Tom Killoran, who was the only senior American diplomat who had worked with all three Angolan movements, firmly believed that the MPLA was in fact the best organized, the most likely to prevail, and ultimately the friendliest to U.S. interests.

Kissinger picked the second option, then decided $6 million didn't sound impressive and cabled Langley from a Paris trip authorizing $14 million. The CIA quickly mobilized to support the FNLA, fighting the MPLA.

Just returned from the evacuation of Saigon, I was ordered to put the CIA's task force together and manage the secret war under the supervision of the CIA's Africa Division chief in Langley and the National Security Council's Interagency Working Group on Angola. One month after we were formally committed to the secret war, I was sent inside Angola to assess the competing forces. I found that Roberto's forces were disorganized and numbered one-hundredth as many as he told us. Savimbi's UNITA forces seemed determined and he was scrupulously honest in the counts and estimates he gave us. We decided to co-opt him into our program.

It should be noted that, at this point, I was skeptical of the CIA and of covert action in general. What I had seen in Vietnam had amounted to a debacle. However I had spent my career out

in the field. I couldn't resist the opportunity to see for myself
how these operations worked from the level of the National
Security Council. I truly hoped I would find that they were
better reasoned and managed than they had seemed. I quickly
abandoned this forlorn soldier's dream.

Throughout the fall of 1975, arms were jammed into Angola, mercenaries were hired, battles were fought, and several
thousand people were killed and wounded. The United States
actively discouraged United Nations and other formal efforts to
mediate. Our budget eventually totalled $31.7 million, a good
part of which was siphoned off into corruption. We encouraged
South African forces to support our Good Guys, while Cuban
soldiers joined the MPLA Baddies.

By winter, the program was thoroughly exposed and the
Congress mercifully passed the Tunney Amendment to the FY
76 Defense Appropriation Bill that ordered our operation closed
down. In the field, our forces had been routed and the MPLA
effectively controlled *all* of the provinces. We had given Jonas
Savimbi the wherewithal to keep the Benguela Railroad closed,
which was our client-state Zaire's only economically viable
egress to the sea for its copper.

We had lied to nearly everyone, lies that were quickly
exposed. Some of those lies to the U.S. Congress, covering up
what we had done, amounted to perjury and could have been
prosecuted as such. We had allied the United States with South
Africa in military activities, which was illegal and impolitic. We
had delivered white mercenaries into Angola to kill blacks as a
technique of imposing our policies on that black African country. Meanwhile, we—not the "Communists"—had interfered
with U.S. commercial interests. We had withdrawn Boeing
Aircraft Corportion's licenses to sell five jetliners to the Angolan
airlines, and we had blackmailed Gulf Oil Company into putting
its $100 million payments in escrow instead of delivering them
to the Bank of Angola. We had poisoned the missionaries' efforts
to run vital schools and hospitals.

Our experience with Gulf Oil Company and Boeing Aircraft Corporation left me with an initial misperception of the
CIA's involvement with multinational corporations. These two

companies were frustrated and inconvenienced by the CIA's secret war in Angola. It cost them money. George Wilson, the President of Boeing, flew to Washington to protest and clear the licenses to sell his airliners to the Angolan government. In my first lectures after leaving the government, I reported that the CIA and the big corporations were, in my own experience, out of step with each other. Later I realized that they may argue about details of strategy—a small war here or there. However, both are vigorously committed to supporting the system. Corporate leaders fight amongst themselves like people in any human endeavor. They raid and hostilely take over each other's companies. Losers have been known to commit suicide. However, they firmly believe in the capitalist system. In two short meetings in Washington, we managed to turn the Boeing President George Wilson around to the point where he sent a letter that we had drafted to the new government of Angola, warning them that the price of crossing the U.S. (secret) government was the loss of access to U.S. technology.

In sum, we had severely damaged U.S. national security interests and nailed our own country with another defeat on the heels of Vietnam.[8]

In one of the classic, ironic follies of intelligence charades, Gulf Oil Company employees returned immediately to resume pumping the Angolan oil—protected militarily by Cuban soldiers from CIA mercenaries who were still marauding and destabilizing the countryside. Nor did the Angola tragedy end with the CIA's defeat in the winter of 1976. Under President Reagan, congressional restraints were lifted and the CIA resumed its support of Jonas Savimbi and his UNITA forces. Over the years the continued destabilization has taken a horrendous toll: the Red Cross counts over 20,000 walking-maimed in Angola today and the central part of the country, which used to be its bread basket, is now a recognized zone of famine.

NICARAGUA

The Nicaragua destabilization is another classic, taken

from the Angola blueprint. The first year of the Nicaraguan operation was almost eerily like the one in Angola. There were three competing factions in each: the leaders in the north, Holden Roberto of the FNLA (in Angola) and Adolfo Calero of UNO (in Nicaragua) were rebarbative characters, while the leaders of the southern movements in each country, Jonas Savimbi (in Angola) and Eden Pastora (in Nicaragua) were remarkably charismatic. In each country, the CIA purchased SWIFT attack launches for coastal operations and put together ragtag air-transport proprietaries. After a couple of years, the Nicaraguan operation began to manifest a substantially different personality. For one thing it became a major artery in drug smuggling, which was not a factor in Angola.

For analytical purposes, the Nicaraguan operation will remain one of the best historical examples because the target country was closer to the United States culturally and geographically, and because the Nicaraguan destabilization was quite open on both ends, i.e., in Washington and in Managua.

Usually these activities are closed—they are *secret*. In most cases our government covers them and hides them to the greatest degree it can, and the country we are attacking becomes hostile and seals its borders to us. Nicaragua, until quite recently, had a policy of remaining open. Anyone from the United States who wanted to go down and have a look could do so without a visa. Meanwhile in Washington the program was debated quite openly as the administration battled for funds and operational details were discussed publicly. Throughout the 1980s, I traveled back and forth from Washington to Nicaragua and elsewhere, informing myself, witnessing and analyzing the operation, and also discussing it in hundreds of lectures.

Nicaragua is unlike Angola in that there never was a chance in Angola that we would make it into another Vietnam, by putting in U.S. troops, whereas this was a very real possibility in Nicaragua during the mid-1980s. The United States has had a fixation on Nicaragua since the mid-1800s. It has long been the ideal site of a possible second canal, better than the Panama canal, connecting the Pacific and Atlantic Oceans, and the target of military intervention. The United States put the Marines into the country half a dozen times early in this century to occupy it, to dominate it, to force elections, to control business interests in that country.

The Marines were eventually withdrawn in 1933 as a result of international pressure, of the international peace movement, and the United States switched to a more subtle form of control than gunboat diplomacy. We created and left behind a National Guard with officers trained in the United States who would be loyal to our interests. This arrangement was the decisive feature of the new era of neocolonialism.

With a brief interruption during World War II, the creation of military oligarchies became a standard U.S. policy of control. We set up schools and eventually trained tens of thousands of military and police officers in countries all over Latin and Central America, in Africa in three cases (Zaire, Ethiopia, and to a lesser extent in Uganda), and in Asia. We put them through our military and police academies, armed them, directly or indirectly paid their salaries when they returned home, and created an international military fraternity of people in power in these countries who were more closely identified with our own military, and hence U.S. national interests and capitalist values, than they were with the people of their own countries.

Meanwhile the cat-and-mouse game that we played with Nicaragua starting in 1981 is a classic case of "destabilization." The strategy, according to the State Department, was to "attack the country's economy." Note how indifferent that sounds from "brutal wreckage" and perhaps you can understand how those people in Washington, most of whom are perfectly decent human beings, can manage activities that cause so much human suffering. It is the magic of rationalization. After all, attacking a *Communist* country's economy was something every patriotic citizen of the United States was expected to applaud every morning before breakfast.

The point of a destabilization is to put pressure on the targeted government by ripping apart the social and economic fabric of the country. These are only words, "social and economic fabric," but what they mean is making the people suffer as much as you can until the country plunges into chaos, until at some point you can step in and impose your choice of government on that country, a strategy that was ultimately successful in the Nicaraguan elections when the people of that country "cried uncle" and voted for the CIA collaborator, Violeta Chamorro.[9] The rationales we used in Nicaragua were classic Cold War slogans: we were "fighting Communism" in the interests of our "national security"; they were a "Marxist bastion in our own backyard"; etc. More specifically, our leaders said at first that the purpose of this program was to "interdict the alleged flow of arms from Nicaragua to the rebels in El Salvador." Unable to prove any flow of arms whatsoever from Nicaragua into El Salvador, the Reagan team, followed eventually by George Bush, developed the propaganda line that they were "returning Nicaragua to democracy." When it was pointed out that Nicaragua had never had a democracy—certainly not under the brutal Somoza dictatorship—they began to speak of the "democratization of Nicaragua," ignoring the fact that Nicaragua had held elections in 1984 that were demonstrably more democratic than the elections that we have in our own Republic.

We will never know exactly what the Sandinistas would have done with Nicaragua if we had left them alone to tackle the country's staggering problems (many of which were the legacy of the Somoza regime) according to their own interests and ideology and compulsions. Everything they did after taking power in 1979 had been in the shadow of U.S. manipulations and covert military attacks on their country. We do know however that there was no blood bath when they took over. They abolished the death sentence at exactly the same time the United States was reinstituting it. The maximum penalty in their courts is 30 years in jail. They released thousands of the hated National Guardsmen that they had in their custody, saying that they would not jail anyone just for having belonged to an organization; the Guardsmen would have to be convicted of individual crimes. This contrasts dramatically with Cuba: when Castro triumphed in 1959, there were a number of executions, generally following trials and sentencing. Of course, the Sandinistas' generosity cost them: many of the Guardsmen they released joined the *contras* in attacking the country.

The Sandinistas launched a literacy campaign to teach every Nicaraguan to read and write and they set out to build 2,500 clinics so Nicaraguans would have access to some kind of medical treatment. These are things that Somoza, the dictator backed by the United States, had not gotten around to doing, and in fact were openly scorned by the dictator and his family.

The first official action taken by the Sandinistas was to establish a ministry of the environment to tackle the damage done under Somoza, who had permitted commercial interests to dump toxic wastes in and thereby "kill" the country's two huge, beautiful lakes. The Sandinistas then launched the most ambitious land reform campaign in the history of Central America. They did this by maintaining a free-enterprise economy with less governmental interference and corruption than Mexico, Peru, or Brazil. Private businessmen could obtain permits, rent an office, install a telephone, and open a business. They could buy land and farm it. If you owned land and you were working it, you kept it. They expropriated the lands that Somoza and his family, and the people who fled, had earned or stolen or taken, and they turned those lands back to the people in cooperatives and different programs, feeling their way, making mistakes as they went, trying this solution and that one, but with the purpose of getting the land back to the people so farmers would own the land, relate to the land, and profit from the land that they worked on in their own country.

In the first four years after the revolution, Nicaragua had the greatest rate of growth of any Latin American country.

The Sandinistas insisted that the church should be a church of the *people,* the church of the poor—not another tool of the oligarchy and the rich and the wealthy. I visited Tomás Borge's office, the Minister of the Interior, and counted the 25 Catholic icon collector items that he had mounted on the wall.

During the Somoza years, Borge was imprisoned and tortured. His wife was imprisoned, raped, tortured, and killed. As Minister of the Interior, he had the men responsible in his power but he did not take revenge on them.

In the 10-year continuous attack—"war" is what the World Court called it—that the United States waged on Nicaragua,

Nicaragua did not commit one act of war against the United States. But instead of joining them in building the healthiest, most dynamic, most enthusiastic country in Central America, the U.S. spent over $1 billion to attack and destabilize the country. We set out systematically to create conditions where farmers could not get their produce to market, where children could not go to school, where women were terrified of being attacked, inside their homes as well as outside, where the hospitals were treating wounded people instead of sick people, where government administration ground to a halt, where the trucks didn't run, the bridges were blown up, the salaries weren't paid, and the infrastructure broke down. Eventually, of course, international capital was scared away and the country plunged into chaos and bankruptcy.

We created the *contra* program beginning in about 1981. Here we go again, said *Newsweek* in November 1982, we have done this before; it has been a mistake before; once again we are supporting the wrong side. We had elected to support the only "truly evil, totally unacceptable faction in the Nicaraguan equation"—the remnants of Somoza's hated *Guardia Nacional* (National Guard). Using Argentine trainers at first, and then eventually CIA mercenaries, we armed and directed this small army from bases mostly in Honduras to attack inside Nicaragua and destabilize the country. They systematically blew up granaries, sawmills, bridges, government offices, schools, health centers, mines. They mined roads, ambushed trucks, and raided farms and villages. There is massive documentation of all this—because, as I said, the country was kept open for foreign witnesses to record what was happening.

For the first few years, CBS, NBC, ABC, BBC, CBC all had crews in Managua, and when there would be atrocities they would rush to film them. We also had what eventually totaled thousands of witnesses for peace from this country, Canada, Europe, and Australia, going down and visiting or even living right in the Nicaraguan towns and villages with the people, and when there were atrocities they filmed and photographed and documented them.

There was also direct U.S. military involvement in mining

harbors, overflying the country, and blowing up installations in the ports. There were assassinations of hundreds of religious leaders, teachers, health workers, elected officials, and government administrators by U.S.-backed *contras.* CBS, NBC, and others have footage of all of this; Americas Watch and Witness for Peace have documented it. There was the admission by President Ronald Reagan in his national television debate with Walter Mondale in 1984 that the famous "assassination manual," used to train the *contras,* was the work of the CIA Station Chief in Tegucigalpa. On national television, Reagan acknowledged the CIA's involvement with the *contras* and in the plotting of assassinations.

After that *faux pas,* the media asked for clarification from the White House on the President's policies. Did President Reagan in fact approve of assassinations, which had been declared at least officially taboo by President Gerald Ford in 1974? In an exercise of doublespeak, the White House said that the word "assassination" only applied to world leaders and chiefs of state. Murdering regional officials was not assassination. The policy, they said was unchanged.

Terror has been a part of this program, terror as raw as anything that happens in the Middle East or elsewhere. The *contras* habitually went into villages and hauled families out of their homes. They forced children to watch while they castrated and killed their fathers, while they raped their mothers and slashed off their breasts, or they forced parents to watch while they mutilated the children.

The *New York Times* has cited 45,000 as the number of people killed and wounded in this destabilization. This is nobody's propaganda. It was all documented and condemned by the World Court, by the Presbyterian Church, by the Methodist Church, by broad segments of the Catholic Church, and by thousands of witnesses who went down from other countries to see for themselves.

Throughout, President Reagan remained unapologetic for this grotesque activity and President Bush continued the same policies. Reagan took pride in saying, "I am a *contra.*" He took pride in saying that these people were the moral equivalent of *his* founding fathers. And of course George Bush has never missed a chance to identify himself with the *contras*.[10]

Destabilization has required a relentless propaganda program to discredit the Sandinistas and label them as totalitarian dictators. At first, we were told that they were flying arms into El Salvador. Then, when the Sandinistas put together a military machine to defend their country from the U.S. attack, we were told that they were building a war machine that "threatened the stability of all of Central America." It was never mentioned that the Nicaraguans did not have strategic weapons and did not have tanks or an air force that could attack other countries, although El Salvador, Honduras, Guatemala, and Panama had been given jet fighter-bombers by the United States.

We charged them with censorship after they closed down the *La Prensa* newspaper. In time it came out that *La Prensa* had been financed by the National Endowment for Democracy and the CIA. This newspaper was owned by the Chamorro family, which means that Violeta Chamorro, victorious in the 1990 elections and supported by George Bush, was a funded collaborator of the CIA during the period when the CIA was directing the brutalization of her country.

Obviously, the United States would never put up with activity like that of *La Prensa* inside its own borders, especially during a war. In fact, there are laws carefully governing our press on the sensitive issues of capitalism. It is very much against the law, for example, for journalists deliberately to print stories that would cause fluctuations on Wall Street, or even to use "insider" information they obtain in their journalistic research to profit from the exchange. Editors of the *Wall Street Journal* have been disciplined for this infraction during the same years that the United States was funding and directing *La Prensa* to create panics inside Nicaragua and castigating the Sandinistas for "censorship."

In 1984, we launched a vigorous campaign to discredit the Nicaraguan elections, elections that were supervised and witnessed by the United Nations and other groups who said that they were as fair as any elections they had seen in Central America in many years. These elections were quite an embarrassment to Ronald Reagan, who was then the champion of the *contra* program, and I am sure to George Bush today, because they were quite a bit more democratic than the elections that we held in this country during the same year, or in 1988. They had seven parties with candidates running for election; the United States had two. They turned out 75.4 percent of the vote; we turned out 53 percent. They voted directly; we voted for electors who selected our leaders. They passed a law that every legitimate party would have an equal subsidy of funds to spend for campaign purposes; in this country if you can raise more money you can buy more television time and you have a much better chance of the winning the election.[11]

Another element of the propaganda program was the claim that they were smuggling drugs to finance their revolution. The CIA staged scenes with the pilot Barry Seales, plea-bargaining a deal with him to land a plane in Panama, to kick some bales of marijuana out on the runway that could be photographed by satellite so President Reagan could put pictures on television saying that it proved the Sandinistas were smuggling drugs. The record, however, proves that the *contras* and their CIA managers were smuggling drugs. There was a massive flow of drugs through the CIA/*contra* aircraft into the United States, where they had clearances to land at Air Force and National Guard bases without being inspected by customs. Senator Kerry's investigation revealed this and there are dozens of cases where people in the *contra* program, including Adolfo Calero's brother-in-law, were caught smuggling cocaine into this country, using informal "national security" passes or telephone numbers from the White House to get themselves cleared when FBI or Drug Enforcement Agency (DEA) officers caught them. This is nothing new. DEA records have been made public revealing that the CIA intervened on behalf of drug dealers at least two dozen times during the 1970s.

The United States also claimed the Sandinistas were responsible for terrorism in Central America, but this case, too, falls flat. The Sandinistas were not involved in terrorist acts—any crimes committed by their soldiers were punished with trials and severe sentences—but the United States has been supporting with literally billions of dollars the activities of armed forces and death squads that were, and still are, slaughtering people in countries like El Salvador and Guatemala. Using the magic of words, U.S. spokespersons like UN Ambassador Jeane Kirkpatrick found a way out. It wasn't "terrorism" if the people responsible for the violence were wearing uniforms provided by U.S. aid.

The United States blamed the Sandinistas for misery in Nicaragua, and the country was (and is) in fact miserable—that was exactly the stated purpose of the U.S. destabilization. The words in Nicaragua are, *"No hay,"* "There isn't any." There are shortages of everything. The country is suffering; its people are suffering. But U.S. Congressional representatives would go down to Managua and have a look and come back and go on television and say, "You won't believe that place; it is the most miserable country I have ever visited. The Sandinistas have not been able to manage it. Look what happens when you have a Marxist government...." To be honest, obviously they would have said, "Our stated purpose back since 1982 was to break the Nicaraguan economy; we spent a billion dollars destabilizing the country to break its economy. Now here are my snapshots of the results of our successful program." Of course, they do not do that because they are playing propaganda. The country is miserable and it was never the fault of the Sandinistas; misery was the stated purpose of the U.S. *contra* destabilization program. One can only imagine what schools and clinics and irrigation projects could have been built with $1 billion.

And then there was "the Soviet threat." For years, President Reagan said that in Nicaragua we had the Soviets and Cubans in our own backyard. He said there were Russians flying airplanes in this hemisphere—meaning into Nicaragua—for the first time in all of history. And like much of what Reagan said—he was never a stickler for accuracy—this was not true. Aeroflot had been flying into Canada, into Mexico, into Latin America, into New York City, for 30 or 40 years on a daily basis, not to mention flying in and out of Cuba continuously.

In the end, the Nicaraguan operation was a bittersweet success for Ronald Reagan. He swore, and failed in this promise, that the Sandinistas would be out of office before he was (after his second term ending in 1989). The Sandinistas were eventually ousted, but under President Bush's watch, after Reagan had retired. Meanwhile, Reagan had seen his presidency virtually destroyed in the Iran/*contra* scandal of 1986.

Moreover, President Reagan had failed in his broader goal. He campaigned his way into office in 1980 by advocating war in many of his speeches. He had assured the nation during and after the 1960s that he would have managed the Vietnam War differently. He promised to restore the nation's confidence in its ability to wage war *and win.* After the invasion of Grenada in October 1983, his constituents sported bumper stickers proclaiming "Nicaragua Next!" "America Feeling Great Again" became the slogan of his 1984 presidential campaign. Meanwhile, the National Guard rehearsed constantly for the invasion of Nicaragua. By the fall of 1986, many respected observers in Washington believed that the date for the invasion had been set for February 1987. There were many indicators. The Pentagon was stirring.

Then, in October 1986, the Iran/*contra* scandal struck. The Reagan administration suffered a number of serious blows: the downing of the Hasenfus plane over Nicaragua, exposure of illegal arms sales to Iran (which had held Americans hostage off and on since the Carter presidency, and quite possibly a decision by the nation's nonpolitical financial managers that an invasion of Nicaragua would have disastrous repercussions throughout Latin America. President Reagan was effectively crippled. He may narrowly have escaped impeachment. Certainly, he no longer had the clout to sell a war to the nation and to a reluctant military establishment.

Still, the national security establishment will record the U.S. destabilization of Nicaragua as a success. In the 1990 elections, Violeta Chamorro, George Bush's friend and long-time CIA collaborator, won. It was a little-publicized fact that the CIA spent about $20 million on those elections to make the people vote to join their tormenters, a pittance after $1 billion that had already been spent to destabilize the country.

Recall the principle of oligarchy through which countries

are controlled since overt colonialism became passé. In order to bring countries like Nicaragua into the loops of international finance, you must have people like Chamorro, who will represent the interest of New York bankers, in power. For this to work, the leaders of the oligarchies have to see some real money themselves. This is why people like the Shah in Iran, Mobutu Sese in Zaire, and Ferdinand Marcos in the Philippines have been permitted to steal billions of dollars from the aid and trade that flows through their countries.[12]

That's why the U.S. establishment is so adamantly against agrarian reform in Third World countries. If you invested $1 billion in a real land reform program in any country, say El Salvador, it would pay off in huge dividends for the people and perhaps return in ten years or so in the form of improved productivity. But if you loan the same $1 billion to the corrupt oligarchy it comes back to you immediately.

In the early 1980s, Morton Halperin of the Center for National Security Studies testified to congressional committees about the decapitalization of El Salvador. For every few million dollars the United States was giving the country in aid, the so-called 14 families were investing a like amount in Miami banks. He quipped that we could save time and effort simply by depositing our aid directly in the rich Salvadorans' Miami bank accounts. The congressmen laughed, but they also voted for more aid to the Salvadoran oligarchy.

OTHER COVERT OPERATIONS

Moving from Nicaragua to the rest of the world, but keeping every aspect of its example in mind as a case study, we have the Church Committee Report of 1975 which revealed that the CIA had been running thousands of operations over the years. Extrapolating the figures as best we can, there have been about 3,000 major covert operations and over 10,000 minor operations—all illegal, and all designed to disrupt, destabilize, or modify the activities of other countries. That is a lot of mischief. Of course, every covert operation has been rationalized in terms of U.S. national security or anti-Communism. Many are now out in the public record. The world is only so big and wars are never completely secret once the fighting begins.

First let me note that many of the thousands of major CIA covert operations were effectively if not literally secret at the time. Even if a few people managed to figure them out, there was little national exposure. The major function of secrecy in Washington is to keep the U.S. people and U.S. Congress from knowing what the nation's leaders are doing. Secrecy is power. Secrecy is license. Secrecy covers up mistakes. Secrecy covers up corruption. A classic non-CIA example was the "secret" bombing of Cambodia in 1970 that eventually became a major political scandal for the Nixon administration. I submit to you that the Cambodian people knew that they were being bombed; it was no secret to them. Unfortunately, there was nothing on the face of the earth that the Cambodian people could do to stop the bombing. However, the people of the United States could stop the bombing, or at least raise an effective protest of it. Hence it was vital to President Nixon that the bombing remain secret here at home.

Other forms of secrecy such as the protection of secret agents overseas or the protection of military-hardware secrets are topics of considerably less concern to our leaders, because they are not likely to become the subjects of domestic dissent. For example, there was an important agent in Vietnam who was the subject of open gossip throughout the official U.S. Embassy community in Saigon. People outside of the CIA—in the Agency for International Development, the U.S. Information Agency— knew a great deal about the operation. The man's life was very much at stake and he was providing invaluable information. When I tried to encourage the chief of station to take measures to suppress the gossip, he and other supergrades only yawned; the agent in question was unlikely to become a political hot potato. On the other hand, I was frequently admonished against talking or even asking about the bugs that the CIA had planted in South Vietnam President Nguyen Van Thieu's office and bedroom. If the first operation became known to the Communists, we would lose an agent but there would be no blowback whatsoever on our managers. However, if the bugs in Thieu's palace were blown to the public, it would be a major scandal and political flap that might cost someone higher up their career.

Three thousand major covert operations, over 10,000 minor operations! Of course the advocates hasten to claim that most of these are neither terribly dramatic nor do they kill or hurt a lot of people. This is probably true. But they are all illegal and they all disrupt the normal functioning, often the democratic functioning, of other societies. They raise serious questions about the moral responsibility of the United States in the international society of nations.

INDONESIA

And many of them are very bloody indeed. For example, in 1965 the CIA organized an operation to discredit the Communist party in Indonesia. Their strategy was to make the party appear to be secretly planning a violent takeover of Indonesian society. The truth was that the Indonesian Communist Party was doing quite well to obtain representation in the Indonesian government through the democratic process. That was what made it so threatening to the United States. They simply could not have an example of legitimate and successful participation by the Communists in the democratic process.

The techniques of the Indonesian destabilization were classic: CIA agents planted caches of arms that would then be "found" by Indonesian police under the watchful eye of the alerted media. Along with the arms would be all kinds of forged documents proving that the Communists were fomenting a violent uprising. Propaganda agents planted stories in the media, inflaming the mistrust of the Communists. Others gave speeches. The situation heated up until some generals in the Indonesian army were killed, and the boil of tension burst. The Indonesian army went after the Communists and the people they felt traditionally supported the Communists. The result was a bloodbath that the *New York Times* described in terms half a million to a million and a half dead. The Australian secret service, closer to Indonesia, put the figure at closer to two million—the rivers were clogged with the bodies of the dead.

In the summer of 1990, the U.S. State Department acknowledged that it had indeed delivered lists of names, of people who were subsequently killed, to the Indonesian government.

The CIA's own internal reporting estimated that 800,000 people had been killed. The organization published a cover story through the Library of Congress that the Communist Party had supported a classic insurrection, which the army had put down. However, internal CIA reports cited the operation as a classic success in which they had targeted the world's third-largest Communist Party and aided the Indonesian army by providing thousands of names of suspected individuals and completely eliminated from the face of the earth not only the party, but the ethnic Chinese in Indonesia who tended to support the Communists. Simply put, this is a classic case of genocide that was engineered by the CIA and cited as a model to be copied elsewhere.[13]

Because of secrecy, we will never know all the details of all the CIA's bloody operations, but we have several hundred of them well documented through congressional investigations, books, and testimony by CIA personnel who were involved, testimony from victims who were tortured and imprisoned, accounts of priests and nuns who were there, and the reporting of journalists covering the events.

To summarize, the CIA has overthrown functioning constitutional democracies in over 20 countries. It has manipulated elections in dozens of countries. It has created standing armies and directed them to fight. It has organized ethnic minorities and encouraged them to revolt in numerous volatile areas.

One of the first things the CIA did in Nicaragua was to give radical elements of the Miskito Indians, who had never gotten along with the other people in Nicaragua, more money than they had ever seen. Then the CIA gave them arms and training and rationales and sanctuaries in Honduras, and sent them into Nicaragua to attack, kill, fight, rape, burn, pillage.

This is insidious. Every society is torn with racial conflicts and conflicts with minorities. Think how volatile our own violent nation is on this subject. Imagine what would happen if there were a super-superpower so big that we did not dare to strike back at them, that funded, armed, and trained African-Americans or Mexican-Americans and sent them into the United States to do open acts of violence. Just think how this nation would rise up, and the bloodbath that would ensue. Home-grown racists still lynch African-Americans when they can get away with it, without any provocation from the outside. Yet stirring up deadly ethnic and racial strife has been a standard technique used by the CIA in Nicaragua, Thailand, Vietnam, Laos, the Congo, Iran, Iraq, and in other parts of the world.

During the 1980s, the CIA created, trained, and funded death squads like the Treasury Police in El Salvador who have been responsible for killing and "disappearing" as many as 70,000 people according to the count of the Catholic Church.

HIDDEN TERRORS

Nothing illustrates the power to rationalize cynicism as well as the Public Safety Program, also called the Office of Public Safety. For about twenty-five years, the CIA, working through the Agency for International Development, trained and organized police and paramilitary officers from around the world in techniques of population control, repression, and torture. Schools were set up in the United States, Panama, and Asia, from which tens of thousands graduated. In some cases, former Nazi officers from Hitler's Third Reich were used as instructors. The program was eventually exposed and an international outcry forced an investigation by the U.S. Congress. A series of laws were passed, officially closing the Public Safety Program down.[14]

The most famous exponent of torture was Dan Mitrione, a former Indianapolis, Ohio, police chief who served seven years in Brazil and three in Uruguay. Eventually he was kidnapped by the people he was targeting and they held him until they had drawn international publicity to their cause; then they killed him. The cat was out of the bag. Researchers and international tribunals investigated his activities and past. Former associates testified.

How does one teach the techniques of torture? There were training films and reading material to supplement lectures on the subject. Eventually, of course, the trainees would have to "get their hands wet." Mitrione would have beggars picked up off the streets and brought in to be used as instructional guinea pigs. Of course, he knew they were not guilty of any untoward activity. They were incapable of saying, "Stop! I'll give you the names of my brothers and sisters." All they could do was lie there and scream. When they would collapse, doctors would be brought in to shoot them up with vitamins to rest them up for the next session. When they would eventually die, their bodies would be mutilated and dropped in the streets to strike fear in the peoples' hearts.

Mitrione eventually became a recognized master in the theories of torture: enough pain to accomplish your purpose, but not enough that shock will protect the victim; never deprive victims of the hope of surviving, else they will give up completely and become inaccessible to the interrogator. A police chief who had worked with Mitrione reported that, after dinner where protocol dictated that the men would separate from the women to have their cigars and cognac, Mitrione would take his guests into a separate room where he had someone locked up, and discuss his theories, while demonstrating some of the techniques.

A woman who was held and tortured in Brazil for two-and-a-half years before she was released because of international protest, testified to various tribunals. She explained that the ultimate horror was that the torturers were *not* raving psychopaths. Had they been, she felt, she might have been able to escape into insanity. Instead, they were sane, normal people, who maintained contact with her mind and kept her present in the room while they tortured her. She recounted a session in which she was lying in a chamber, naked, on a table, in a room with a half-dozen men who were doing incredibly painful and degrading things to her body. There was an interruption; the

American was called to the telephone and the others took a smoke break. She listened while the American chatted with his wife about wrapping things up in a couple of hours and then picking up the children on his way home.

Dan Mitrione too was a stable family man, a devout Catholic, a devoted father, a respected member of the U.S. embassy communities in which he lived and worked. And yet he had dedicated his life to torturing people, some of whom he knew were innocent of any crime, because his society had agreed that there was something so sacred about "national security" that it transcended all humane considerations. It justified even torture. Note that the American people, the Congress, even his presidents, at least tacitly supported his activities. The Vice-President of the United States attended his funeral in order to uplift his family and all his colleagues, who might have doubts about what he had done with his life.

CHILE

Twice in the 1960s, the CIA spent large sums of money to influence the outcome of elections in Chile and to install a president of the United States' choosing. Eventually it failed and democracy prevailed in the election of President Salvador Allende Gossens. Under the direction of President Nixon, the CIA organized the famous Track I and Track II destabilization of Chile in order to oust Allende. CIA Deputy Director for Operations, Richard Helms (who later became CIA Director) testified before the Congressional Oversight Committee and lied. He was later indicted for lying to the Congress about the Chilean operation and plea-bargained a suspended sentence and a fine, which the association of CIA exes paid for him. Finally, he offered a copy of the notes he had made in the National Security Council meeting in the White House where he was ordered to mount the Chilean operation. He had jotted down the following instructions: "Make the Chilean economy scream." He testified that when he returned to CIA headquarters at Langley to give his staff their marching orders, even they were dumfounded at the cynicism of the operation. Helms told them, "Gentlemen, let's not sit around wringing our hands. We've been given a job to do."

With the help of the U.S. military, which had solid connections with the Chilean military through the American-sponsored international military fraternity, and with the help of certain multinational corporations like ITT, the CIA mounted the successful operation to oust the democratically-elected president of Chile, who was killed in the process. At one point prior to the coup, General René Schneider, the pro-U.S. head of the Chilean military, was an obstacle because he was stubbornly supporting democracy and the constitutional process. So they killed him too and installed the monster Pinochet in power. About 30,000 people were killed by Pinochet, whose secret police were so violent that they even engineered bombings in our own nation's capital. It took the best effort of the Chilean people, eventually with diplomatic help from the United States, to undo the damage and return the country to a democratic process 16 years later.

When Henry Kissinger was grilled by the Congress about the Chilean operation, he had this to say: "Yes, the issues are much too important for the Chilean voters to be left to decide for themselves."

THE KOREAN WAR

CIA operations have also led our nation into war. There was, for example, a long CIA destabilization and propaganda campaign against China after the triumph of Mao Tse Tung in 1949 and the ouster of General Chiang Kai-shek, whom the United States had supported. The United States installed Chiang and his Koumintang party in Taiwan, and the CIA mounted a massive operation, parachuting teams from Quemoy, Matsu, Tibet, Burma, and Thailand, to destabilize mainland China much as the *contras* did in Nicaragua 30-odd years later. I remember instructors in my own CIA training classes, who had been part of that operation, telling us over drinks at happy hour how they would sometimes tie-off the parachutes of agents they didn't like or trust so they would "cream in" (i.e., die) when they jumped out of planes over China.

Part of this operation was an ineffectual propaganda campaign directed at the people of mainland China. Another part was the highly successful propaganda campaign aimed at the people of the United States, designed to make them see Mao in the worst possible light and to support the brutal and corrupt Chiang. Eventually, this operation resulted in the Korean War where we fought China in Korea, and in which one million people were killed.[15]

THE VIETNAM WAR

There was also a long CIA destabilization and propaganda campaign against Vietnam before we talked ourselves into the Vietnam War in which two million people were killed. The history of this operation dates back, ironically, to World War II, when U.S. intelligence was working with Ho Chi Minh in the jungles of Vietnam to rescue downed U.S. pilots. After the Japanese fled Southeast Asia in early 1945, before their impending defeat, Ho Chi Minh read a declaration of Vietnamese independence in Hanoi that directly quoted the American Declaration of Independence, that in fact the OSS (Office of Strategic Services, the CIA's World War II predecessor) officer Archimedes Patti had helped him write. Patti stood beside him as he read his declaration. Ho Chi Minh wrote six letters to President Harry Truman assuring him of friendship and asking for support. They were never answered.

Unfortunately, the French were eager to restore their colonial empire in Vietnam, and the United States opted to stand by its Western ally rather than support the newly independent republic of Vietnam. Despite Ho's nationalism and friendship for the United States, he was also a "Communist" and this was exactly the moment in history when the United States was formulating the anti-Communist rationales for the Cold War. Ho had to be listed with the Bad Guys.

For seven years, the United States supported the French in their war against Ho's forces, providing them with military aid and even contemplating the use of nuclear weapons to relieve them in the siege of Dienbienphu. When the French were defeated there in 1954, the United States stepped into the vacuum, and its Vietnam adventure was launched. The Geneva Accords that partitioned the country into northern and southern zones, from which the United States abstained, provided for elections in 1956 in which the Vietnamese people would decide for themselves on questions of unity and leadership. However, the United States quashed those elections—President Eisenhower himself admitted that he could not allow the elections to happen because 80 percent of the people would have voted for Ho Chi Minh.

Instead, the CIA plunged into the breach with a massive covert operation. In Hanoi, anti-Communist propaganda was disseminated to terrify the population. The propaganda campaign targeted the Vietnamese Catholic community in particular. One story that was widely disseminated was that Communists had gone into a Catholic maternity hospital and killed 1,000 pregnant mothers. Stamps were carefully forged and put on letters that allegedly came from Hanoi, advocating violence and attacks on the West. At the same time efforts were made to disrupt the economy: abrasives, for example, were added to the oil that was delivered to Hanoi in order to destroy buses' transmissions and cripple vital public transportation. A junk full of arms was crashed onto the coast of South Vietnam, and journalists were flown in by the U.S. mission (in cooperation with the CIA) to witness and record this "flagrant evidence" of Ho's attack on the South.

The Catholic population in Hanoi panicked and fled south—the U.S. Navy happened to be standing by to haul 800,000 of them away. In Saigon, they provided the giant nucleus of an instant, pro-U.S. oligarchy. The United States provided them with huge amounts of aid and the CIA flew in the exiled priest, Ngo Dinh Diem, to run South Vietnam. The CIA station chief met Diem at the airport and a CIA-recruited staff of trusted Filipinos was waiting for him at the presidential palace.

French intelligence, in collaboration with the Sicilian Mafia, had run an arms-for-drugs operation in the Vietnamese and Laotian mountains. The CIA station chiefs in Saigon, Ed Lansdale and then Three-fingered Lou Conein, sorted out initial problems with the Sicilians as the CIA took over the operation. The CIA's proprietary airlines, Civil Air Transport and then Air America, took over the flights of arms and drugs. The French-born Conein was awarded the Napoleon Eagle and the Corsican Cross, which, he boasted, gave him access to the Mafia's inner-most councils.

Meanwhile, Conein was running a *contra*-type operation in which 90 teams were sent into North Vietnam to destabilize the country. This program was a failure; the teams were all captured and neutralized. In time, the Diem presidency failed too. Diem simply would not play ball with the United States and his corruption and brutality alienated the Buddhist south to the point where monks began to immolate themselves, inflaming world opinion. So in 1963, the CIA encouraged a *coup d'état* in which Diem and his brother were killed. A succession of candidates was shuffled in and out of the South Vietnamese presidency until the CIA settled on Nguyen Van Thieu who remained President until the CIA helped him escape from Saigon as South Vietnam collapsed in 1975.

By early 1963, President Kennedy had begun to realize that Vietnam was a trap in which the United States would only become hopelessly entangled, and he decided to withdraw U.S. forces from the country. This may have been one of the reasons he was eliminated by assassination in Dallas in November 1963.

President Johnson accepted the Vietnam War as a compromise with the conservative forces in the States, a trade-off for his program of liberal domestic reforms, called the Great Society. The problem, of course, was how to elicit popular support for a massive escalation of the war. The groundwork had been laid for a 10-year propaganda campaign aimed at the American public to orchestrate support for the war effort, just as support for the Korean War had been managed 15 years earlier. All that was needed was a trigger, and that was conveniently provided by a CIA naval unit in Vietnam that was so secret the United States had not even advised South Vietnamese authorities of its existence.

After midnight on July 30, 1964, Norwegian-built "SWIFTS" or "NASTIES," manned with CIA crews, attacked the North Vietnamese radar station on Hon Me Island and bombarded Hon Ngu in the Gulf of Tonkin. The North Vietnamese sent a formal protest to the United States. The frigate USN *Maddox*, which was patrolling inside North Vietnamese waters to provide cover for the CIA marauders, remained on station. Clearly provoked and pursuing the CIA marauders, North Vietnamese moved to challenge the *Maddox*. The *Maddox* fired first; the Vietnamese answered with torpedoes that missed. A garbled version of the incident, blaming the North Vietnamese, was trumpeted through a cooperative media to the U.S. public and was used to justify formal moves by Lyndon Johnson to launch the Vietnam War (which had been in open planning stages for two years). The rest is history.[16]

Coming to grips with these U.S./CIA activities in broad numbers and figuring out how many people have been killed in the jungles of Laos or the hills of Nicaragua is very difficult. But, adding them up as best we can, we come up with a figure of six million people killed—and this is a minimum figure. Included are: one million killed in the Korean War, two million killed in the Vietnam War, 800,000 killed in Indonesia, one million in Cambodia,[17] 20,000 killed in Angola—the operation I was part of—and 22,000 killed in Nicaragua. These people would not have died if U.S. tax dollars had not been spent by the CIA to inflame tensions, finance covert political and military activity, and destabilize societies.

Certainly, there are other local, regional, national and international factors in many of these operations, but if the CIA were tried fairly in a U.S. court, under U.S. law, the principle of complicity, incitement, riot, and mayhem would clearly apply. In the United States, if you hire someone to commit a murder your sentence may be approximately the same as that of the murderer himself.

Who are these six million people we have killed in the

interest of American national security? Conservatives tell us, "It's a dangerous world. Our *enemies* have to die so we can be safe and secure." Some of them say, "I'm sorry, but that's the way the world is. We have to accept this reality and defend ourselves, to make our nation safe and insure our way of life."

Since 1954, however, we have not parachuted teams into the Soviet Union—our number one enemy—to destabilize that country. (Coincidentally, 1954 was the first year the Soviets developed the capability of actually dropping atomic weapons on the United States.) Neither do we run these violent operations in England, France, Sweden, Norway, Belgium, or Switzerland. Since the mid-1950s they have all been conducted in Third World countries where governments do not have the power to force the United States to stop its brutal and destabilizing campaigns.

One might call this the "Third World War." It is a war that has been fought by the United States against the Third World. Others call it the Cold War and focus on the anti-Communist and anti-Soviet rationales, but the dead are not Soviets; they are people of the Third World. It might also be called the Forty-Year War, like the Thirty-Year and Hundred-Year Wars in Europe, for this one began when the CIA was founded in 1947 and continues today. Altogether, perhaps twenty million people died in the Cold War. As wars go, it has been the second or third most destructive of human life in all of history, after World War I and World War II.

The six million people the CIA has helped to kill are *people* of the Mitumba Mountains of the Congo, the jungles of Southeast Asia, and the hills of northern Nicaragua. They are people without ICBMs or armies or navies, incapable of doing physical damage to the United States. The 22,000 killed in Nicaragua, for example, are not Russians; they are not Cuban soldiers or advisors; they are not even mostly Sandinistas. A majority are rag-poor peasants, including large numbers of women and children.

Communists? Hardly, since the dead Nicaraguans are predominantly Roman Catholics. Enemies of the United States? That description doesn't fit either, because the thousands of witnesses who have lived in Nicaraguan villages with the people since 1979 testify that the Nicaraguans are the warmest people on the face of the earth, that they love people from the United States, and they simply cannot understand why our leaders would want to spend $1 billion on a *contra* force designed to murder people and wreck the country.

WHY SECRET WARS?

Glasnost is not intended to benefit the Third World, nor will it. The Soviet Union has never been a world leader in terms of racial sensitivity or concern for the Third World peoples' interests. The impetus behind *glasnost* was the collapse of the Soviet Union's archaic Stalinist system and its grievous economic problems.

Glasnost is a strategy to unite the first world against the Third World. Soviet President Gorbachev has called for global economic "stability" in the interests of world trade and greater credibility for the Soviet Union. More concretely, Soviet attack helicopters, designed for fighting a war in Afghanistan, are being used today in joint operations with U.S. and Peruvian military who strafe and rocket villagers in attacks on drug smugglers and "Shining Path" revolutionaries in Peru.

President Gorbachev has recently agreed with President George Bush that Soviet and U.S. military would join forces against Iraq under UN auspices if the Persian Gulf crisis erupts into war. Remember, George Bush prepared the way for this historic cooperation when, en route to his September 1990 meeting with Gorbachev in Helsinki, he asserted that "we now have the opportunity to establish a new world order."

Why would the United States spend billions of dollars to destabilize every corner of the globe for four or five decades? Economics is one reason, but not at the level many people suspect. An excellent film in the mid-1980s, titled *Destination Nicaragua,* suggested that the U.S. *contra* program was motivated by competition for Nicaraguan exports and even its domestic market. After spending time in Nicaragua, I concluded that this didn't make sense. For one thing, Nicaragua exports coffee and cotton, two commodities so overproduced that quotas must be assigned to countries to keep the world prices up. Nor does Nicaragua have enough money or people to be a noticeable market for U.S. goods, and our goods generally are not competitive with those from Korea, Taiwan, and Singapore anyway. Even if the United States had exclusive access to

85

Nicaraguan markets and produce, it would take 100 years for the United States to recover the $1 billion-plus that it spent to destabilize the country during the 1980s. Moreover, simple arithmetic reveals that, had $1 billion been spent to build irrigation and health projects in Nicaragua, the United States might well have reaped some profits from such an investment.

One real economic motive behind the Third World War is the $150 billion drug trade, which speaks for itself. This money is not lost to the international banking world. It is laundered through Panamanian and Caribbean banks and put right back into global circulation.

The major economic impetus behind the Third World War, however, is the production of arms. Every day $3 billion worth of weapons is bought and sold. So-called defense corporations are making 20-25 percent profit. In the 1980s, the United States spent a total of $2.5 trillion (at least those were the announced figures, the total was probably much greater) on the largest arms buildup perhaps in the history of the world and certainly of any country during peacetime. The country's debt increased by almost exactly the same amount during that period.

This was a continuation of a post-World War II system, dominated by what President Eisenhower called the "military-industrial complex." The U.S. taxpayer is now carrying a gigantic burden. Nearly one-third of the nation's budget goes to the military. According to studies published in the *Washington Post*, 53 cents of every tax dollar goes to the military to pay for arms, salaries, facilities, overhead, and debts from Vietnam and other wars.

OUR MILITARISTIC CULTURE

Although the United States promotes itself as a "peace-loving nation," the United States in fact has a history of constant wars. In our 200-plus-year history, we have fought 15 wars. We have put our military into other countries to force them to bend to our will about 200 times, or about once a year. If you review the history of these wars and invasions, you will find that U.S.

leaders almost always cited protection of national interests, or the protection of U.S. lives and property (at the expense of the local peoples' lives and property) as the justification. As early as 1836, President Andrew Jackson called the war against the Seminole Indians a war of "national defense."

In each war there was a "trigger," i.e., an incident that was seized upon or sometimes engineered and then used to galvanize the public into supporting the war. The orchestration of public opinion before the war against Mexico in 1846 provides an excellent case study. At first, U.S. leaders offered $2 to any soldier who would volunteer. Then they offered 100 acres of land, but still did not get enough volunteers. When all else had failed, they sent Zachary Taylor with a small force to raid up and down the Mexican side of the border until Mexican forces responded, and then they were able to trumpet the headlines to the nation: "Mexicans Killing Our Boys In Texas." The nation rose up in support of the war, enabling the United States to annex territory that would eventually become New Mexico, Arizona, California, and part of Colorado.

President Franklin Roosevelt worked carefully and persistently to move the country away from isolationism and into support of the British in World War II. British intelligence and some high U.S. officials, including President Roosevelt, were aware of Japanese intentions to attack Pearl Harbor. They were tracking the Japanese fleet as it crossed the pacific. However, they studiously did nothing; they did not even warn the admirals and generals in Pearl Harbor of the impending attack. The fleet was left, a sitting duck, in the sheltered port where on December 7, 1941, it was sunk with the loss of over 2,000 lives of U.S. servicemen. President Roosevelt was on the radio immediately trumpeting the "Day of Infamy" and the nation rallied behind him in the war effort. *They sacrificed the U.S. fleet and a substantial number of sailors' and soldiers' lives in order to have their casus belli!* After the war, having done their duty and kept their silence, the U.S. admirals involved in the Pacific published a joint article bitterly faulting Roosevelt for not having alerted the Navy in Pearl Harbor, and for leaving the fleet at anchor where it could be destroyed.

The Vietnam War was triggered by the Gulf of Tonkin incident which was provoked, then distorted, by President Lyndon Johnson as he plunged the nation into war (discussed in greater detail below). The bombing of Libya in April 1986 was "justified" by a distorted incident in Germany. The invasion of Grenada in September 1983 was justified by the alleged threat to U.S. citizens' lives (although the citizens were not in danger and their safety had been guaranteed by the Grenadan leaders.) The sinking of the *Lusitania* justified the U.S. entry into World War I; the sinking of the *Maine* justified the Spanish Cuban American War. More recently, the CIA has been busy destabilizing Iraq, contributing significantly to the Iraqi invasion of Kuwait and the *casus belli* in the Persian Gulf.

We begin conditioning our children to war at very tender ages. When we put our children in front of the television and turn it on so we can go wash the dishes or take a break, and they watch the same show, with different characters, 10 or 15 times a day—that's when it begins. I have a young child, so I'm aware that He-man, Sheena, the Thundercats, the Transformers and the Decipticons, Mr. T, and even Scooby-Doo all have the same plot: nice, handsome, light-skinned people are put upon by ugly evil forces. The Good Guys always say, "Please be nice." The Bad Guys—like Skeletor who is dark, ugly, and evil—insist on attacking, and at the last minute the Good Guys rise up and blow them away. Cut, commercial, and they move on to the next show, until we graduate from high school, when it is estimated that we have literally spent more time watching violence on television than we have spent in the classrooms. I call this view our children are given of ourselves as the Good Guys of the world "The American Syndrome."

Television is not the only prop of our militaristic culture. Hollywood movies also fed us a military buildup during the 1980s: *Rambo, Commando, Red Dawn,* the *Rocky* series, *Under Siege, Delta Force, Amerika, Missing in Action, Top Gun, Heartbreak Ridge, Death Before Dishonor, Platoon, Hamburger Hill, Tour of Duty, Robocop, Lethal Weapon*—the list goes on and on.

Red Dawn was especially interesting because its producer went on television to announce that his purpose was to make a movie that would draw people back to war—that would make people feel war could be a good and exciting thing. The film was actually shown in Marine boot camps to motivate people, and to National Guard units that were about to go down to train in Honduras for the possible invasion of Nicaragua.

The scenario—science fiction, of course—is that a force of Russians, Cubans, and Nicaraguans has invaded the United States, and they have gotten all the way to the Rocky Mountains. There is no explanation of what has happened to the U.S. military, or to its 25,000 thermonuclear weapons, or of the fact that the Soviets do not have a dominant navy with a remarkable capability for long-range, massive landings.

Why did the producers pick Russians, Cubans, and Nicaraguans? Wouldn't *Red Dawn* have been more compelling if it had been about Russians, *Canadians,* and *Mexicans*? Canada is an industrial country that shares a huge border with the United States. Isn't it more likely that the Russians would come across at 100 places and pin us against Mexico? Why pick Nicaragua and Cuba instead?The answer of course is that Cuba is a notorious, designated enemy which the U.S. national security establishment was targeting, along with Nicaragua, for possible military action. (Remember, Secretaries of State Al Haig and George Shultz both advocated U.S. military action; Haig had urged the U.S. to "go to the source," namely Cuba.) This film was produced by a public supporter of President Reagan's aggressive policies. Nor should the reader forget that Reagan was a product of Hollywood, with a strong following there that included Charleton Heston, Tom Selleck, Clint Eastwood, and many lesser lights. Ronald Reagan and his backers spoke openly and with great satisfaction of their successful "Reagan Revolution" which intended to restore popular acceptance of war and to condition viewers to see Cubans and Nicaraguans as dangerous enemies.

In the movie, the combined Russian, Cuban, and Nicaraguan invasion force gets all the way to the Rocky Mountains, where it is finally stopped by a high school football team. Question: why did they cast teenagers as the nation's saviors? Weren't there any adults around who could be trusted with such a tough assignment? The answer is obvious: they are going to fight the next war with the 18-year-olds and 19-year-olds just as they have done throughout history. Those of us in middle age or older tend to be more skeptical. We have seen the cynicism of war; we wouldn't buy it. It's the high school graduates, the young men suffering from "testosterone poisoning," conditioned since they were two years old to see violence as noble, who have not yet had time to defend themselves, *to defend their minds.* They do not yet have the experience and knowledge to understand what the world is all about and see how they can be used. Hence, they were easy targets for *Red Dawn.*

This cynicism is as old as U.S. history, as old as history itself. In 1915, Kate Richards O'Hare said, "The women of the United States are nothing but brood sows, having sons to be put into the army and made into fertilizer." She was jailed for five years for anti-war talk, which was illegal.

Think about the ads on television—"Join the Army. Be all that you can be"—that show tanks jumping ditches, and helicopters going 200 miles per hour, with computers and lasers like the Nintendo war training games that are used to hypnotize our ten-year-olds. We didn't have tanks like that when I was in the Marine Corps. Our tanks would run over a very small ditch and break down. And the helicopters went 80 miles per hour and there were no computers. But what is really missing in these commercials? Where are the young men and women with their legs blown off at the knees, with their intestines wrapped around their necks, the little girls running down the road, on fire, human torches covered with napalm? These commercials are not meant to educate. They are part of how we are conditioning them, reaching inside their breasts and pressing buttons and manipulating them to "join the Army and be all that you can be," insuring their availability to be sent down to Central America to kill people and die for our country. It's almost unnecessary to note that these ads are paid for with our tax dollars. No ads are paid for with our tax dollars that urge people not to join the Army or encourage them to reject the military machine.

Taking smoothly over from the arcade games, which are nearly all violent, our society feeds its youth on the great military conditioning program of football, complete with the captain (coach), the sargeant (quarterback), and troops.

One of the most insidious ads in the history of television is of a handsome young soldier coming home on leave. He is met by his brother—I think he is getting off a train—and he says, "Dad never did understand why I joined the Army." Then they are driving and he asks, "Do you think he will ever forgive me?" The younger brother answers, "Well, you know Dad." When they arrive home, the young soldier says, "Dad," and the father turns and hugs him, and all is forgiven. What is the point? This ad cost many millions of dollars. It was produced by a big-time ad agency. There must have been a carefully devised purpose. The problem they are addressing in this ad is that there are a lot of fathers in this country who are saying, "Do not join the Army." Fathers today are in a position to have seen the Vietnam War and the Korean War; they have seen the cynicism and they are telling their sons *not* to join the Army. This ad is saying that it is okay to defy your father and join the Army, that he will forgive you and eventually embrace you if you do.

This romantic, idealized conditioning of our children to war (reminiscent of the ancient Spartans, and other militaristic cultures of the past) is essential to the functioning of our permanent war complex, but it is also a two-edged sword. People grow up and taste the truth. After nearly every one of our wars, including the "Good War" (World War II wherein Hitler and the Japanese leaders were so demonstrably evil that the rationales were ironclad), the nation has had to deal with embittered veterans who realized how they had been used. After World War II, the discerning ones found that big business had built the airplanes for the Germans and supplied the fuel and ball bearings that had bombed them in the battle for Europe. During and after the Vietnam War, most veterans and many others in the nation perceived the cynicism and waste of their lives and the lives of two million Vietnamese.

I consider this romantic, childhood conditioning very much responsible for the tragedy of my own life, in which I devoted my prime to the service of what anti-nuclear activist Helen Caldicott aptly calls "the white male killer establishment."

In all fairness, we must note that women are not at all immune to the politics and rationales of war. Prominent modern women leaders—Golda Meir, Indira Gandhi, and Margaret Thatcher—have led their countries into wars. In September 1990, Texas gubernatorial candidate Ann Richards, although a Democrat and far more progressive than the above named "iron ladies," made a show of taking a press pool with her as she went to shoot doves in South Texas, in a pathetic effort to appease the National Rifle Association lobby and demonstrate that she was as macho as her notoriously insensitive competitor, Clayton Williams.

THE ECONOMIC FUNCTION OF DESTABILIZATION

The lesson of the runaway arms race, with its giant expenditures on the military, is that the nation has gone deeply, irreversibly into debt, and every conceivable social service is being sacrificed. We cannot afford guns *and* butter. To pay for the arms race the nation has to cut thousands of social programs, as was done under President Reagan, as continues under George Bush. The nation cannot go wild on military expenditures and also afford to care for old people, poor people, disabled people, farmers, or students.

This is why Joe Clark, the tough-talking high school principal, is the darling of the arms advocates, why he is the star of the exquisitely well-done movie *Lean On Me,* which makes him into a hero as he teaches people to pull themselves up by their bootstraps, not to depend on the government for funds for schools or other facilities. The man is a fascist: bullying, beating, and humiliating people, but the movie claims it's all for the greater good. Even when he breaks reasonable fire ordinances, he is forgiven and 3,000 students march to cheer him at the jail. (This is an obvious parallel to Oliver North, Ronald Reagan, and George Bush, in the Iran/*contra* scandal.) The woman on welfare is insulted, another down-and-out woman finds a job (there is no indication of retraining her for better work), and the pregnant girl is blamed by the jerk principal. In the end, the woman who has been organizing within the system to fight for improved conditions, but with principles, is called a "loud-mouthed witch" and fades away while a mob laughs and cheers.

Currently the government is counting Social Security revenues as income against the uncontrolled deficits. We are supposed to get that money back when we are 65. Now the government is eyeing our retirement pension as if it were windfall profits to cover the deficit that it has accumulated in the production of arms. Real deficits are running about $385 billion, but our leaders are acknowledging only $152 billion, part of the difference being drawn against the Social Security Retirement Fund that belongs to us.

The result is that the United States has plummeted, relative to the rest of the industrialized world, from its pinnacle of wealth and economic strength. Twenty-five percent of the people in this country are now functionally illiterate. We are sixth in the world in terms of the percentage of children in school; seventh in life expectancy; tenth in quality of education; tenth in quality of life standards; and twentieth in infant mortality.

To sell these sacrifices to the American people, the world must *be* hostile and dangerous. Hence the title of my first book, *In Search of Enemies,* and the thesis of this book. Enemies are necessary for the wheels of the U.S. military machine to turn. If the world were peaceful, we would never put up with this kind of ruinous expenditure on arms at the cost of our own lives. This is where the thousands of CIA destabilizations begin to make a macabre kind of economic sense. They function to kill people who never *were* our enemies—that's not the problem—but to leave behind, for each one of the dead, perhaps five loved ones who are now traumatically conditioned to violence and hostility toward the United States. This insures that the world will continue to be a violent place, populated with *contras* and Cuban exiles and the armies in Southeast Asia, justifying the endless, profitable production of arms to "defend" ourselves in such a violent world.

Since the end of World War II, the Soviet Union has been held up to us as the "evil empire," but that hasn't been enough. It has been too far away, and direct conflict would have brought the world to Armageddon. In order to have periodic wars, there had to be lesser, non-nuclear enemies. These have been designated variously over the years: China, Cuba, Vietnam, and Nicaragua, for example.

Nicaragua is the best recent case of a primary designated enemy during the historic arms build-up of the Reagan years. In fact, President Reagan spent more public presidential energy addressing his *contra* program against Nicaragua than any other aspect of his presidency. You recall the lines he used at various times: "...a Communist beachhead right in our own backyard..." "...there are now Soviets flying planes in this hemisphere for the first time in history..." "...the creeping virus of Communism..." "...it's a two-day drive from Managua to Harlingen, Texas..." "...it's closer from Managua to Houston than from Houston to Maine...." "...there will be a million Communists coming up across our borders from Central America...."

Wow! Man the trenches! This propaganda, obviously, is transparent. It takes most of us who live in Texas about a week to drive from Harlingen to Managua, if you have a reliable car and can get through safely. However, Reagan was in fact successful in using Nicaragua as a designated enemy to cultivate paranoia and support for his huge expenditure on arms.

Conservative intellectuals admit the harshness of U.S. counter-revolutionary activities but argue that they are necessary. They claim that the system has worked for 200 years to make the United States the most powerful country in the world. They know that people die by the thousands in these activities, but claim that they are nevertheless necessary to maintain U.S. security and the U.S. standard of living.

DOMESTIC MANIPULATIONS

It would be asking far too much of human nature to expect that individuals who have run operations overseas that included everything from illegal mischief to the depraved and genocidal to return to the United States and restrain themselves. Most of them believe in what they are doing. They have been armed by their leaders and they have armed themselves with rationales that provide plausible denial to their own consciences. Overseas, they are saving other countries from the Communist menace and now other threats. How can they be expected to resist also trying to "save" the United States as well? And the leaders, most of whom are well aware of the broader cynicism of which they are a part, are as eager to control the United States itself as they are to manipulate the destinies of far away places. Whatever the legal restraints, it is clear that they have run countless, illegal operations inside the United States as well.

An obvious example is the Iran/*contra* scandal of the 1980s, in which a dozen laws were broken in illegal sales of arms, mercenary activity, illegal acts of war (that were condemned by the World Court), drug smuggling, perjury, and circumventing congressional restrictions by setting up an "off-the-shelf" program in which the CIA Director William Casey, Oliver North, and various other individuals "wired around" the CIA's built-in controls and its legalistic officers (of which there are plenty). They paid speakers to travel around the nation advocating the cause of the *contras*; they targeted and maligned politicians who were opposed to the program.

This activity, and in fact most CIA activity, would not be possible were it not for a inherent and sometimes difficult to understand complicity from the major organs of the media. Orchestrations to war would never work if the media were more vigilant—if they did not cooperate with the national security establishment. Ben Bagdikian, Noam Chomsky, Edward Herman, Michael Parenti, and Martin Lee have all published useful studies on the subject. Media politics is also the focus of Fairness and Accuracy in Reporting (FAIR), an organization in New York

City that has published, among other things, important studies documenting the political biases of Ted Koppel's "Nightline."

The First Amendment does not require anyone to publish the truth, just as there is no law requiring politicians to tell their constituents the truth (although there are laws requiring that constituents not to lie to the politicians). Who is to decide what the truth is? The First Amendment guarantees everyone's right to publish anything they want, from whatever bias and slant they choose.

While there are innumerable conscientious journalists who are eagerly probing for facts and reporting them, the major organs of the media are themselves literally multinational corporations. The people who sit on the Board of Directors of the *New York Times,* CBS, or the *Washington Post* also sit on the boards or have interest in defense and other major multinational corporations. NBC is actually owned by General Electric, which is one of the largest defense contractors. While the owners of the major newspapers do not and in fact cannot meddle heavily in the daily running of their organs—sooner or later the readers would become incensed and wouldn't buy their newspapers—they certainly hire and fire the editors who do. And by the time an individual acquires enough seniority to become an editor, he or she generally does not have to be coached on a daily basis.

The owners and editors of major news organs are well aware of the power they wield and they consciously exercise it. We have abundant examples: Clare Booth Luce of the powerful Lucepress conglomerate was firmly and openly committed to the destabilization of Fidel Castro's Cuba in the 1960s. She enjoyed having Cuban exiles associated with CIA's OP-MONGOOSE program into her home for visits. The owners of the *Washington Post* long ago acknowledged that the *Post* is the government's voice to the people. In 1981, Katherine Graham, who owns the *Washington Post* and *Newsweek* announced that her editors would "cooperate with the national security interests." National security in this context means "CIA." This is what Bob Woodward's book, *Veil: The Secret Wars of the CIA* is really about, namely the symbiotic relationship between the *Washington Post* and the CIA. Every time he dug up a story about

CIA activities, he and the *Post's* editors called CIA Director William Casey to consult with him about its publication. They did not always agree with his reaction, but they always called.

In 1984, the *Washington Post* and then the *New York Times* reported that *New York Times* reporter Leslie Gelb had cooperated with the CIA under the Carter administration in 1978 to recruit journalists in Europe who would publish stories that would encourage readers to be sympathetic to the development of the neutron bomb. In 1975, the Church Committee of the Senate found that there existed an intimate (and unholy) relationship between the CIA and editors and journalists at every level. Several hundred people in the media cooperate with the CIA, some as paid agents, some on a *quid pro quo* information-sharing basis (You run this story for me and I'll give you three "scoops" of information your competitors do not have.) Some, like Graham and Luce, are ideological fellow-travellers who believe in the CIA's missions; others are members of the same Old Boy network.

In my own book, *In Search of Enemies,* I outlined how we in the CIA's Angola program created a mechanism whereby we could feed stories to the media like an intravenous needle and tube in a patient's arm. One has no difficulty finding journalists who will cooperate. The problem is how they will explain their stories, say about what is happening inside Angola, to their fiercely competitive colleagues while in fact residing in Paris or New York. To solve this problem, we put CIA officers who were media specialists at key locations around Angola. We obtained approval from the presidents of two countries to plant, through UNITA and FNLA cut-outs, our stories in their primary newspapers. Then—the key—we recruited and hired local stringers who would telex the articles to our controlled agents in Europe and elsewhere. The latter had solid, visible proof of the source of our propagandistic articles. Note, this system would nevertheless not withstand intense scrutiny. It would work as long as we were writing on acceptable themes, like (fictional) Cuban rapists inside Angola, but not if we were skinning any of the establishment's sacred cows.

CIA activities have left a permanent mark on life inside the

United States as well. In the MKULTRA program, the CIA, working with the U.S. Army and Navy for well over twenty years, experimented on witting and unwitting people in the United States and abroad with disease and drugs. We do not have all the details of this lengthy operation, but what we do know is chilling. The roots of MKULTRA may go back to Nazi Germany's macabre experiments on human guinea pigs during World War II, when the reports of their findings were shamelessly republished in prestigious U.S. medical journals.

The pro-CIA book by John Ranelagh, *The Agency*, which collects the memoirs of CIA founders Larry Houston, Jack Pforzheimer, Ray Cline, and others, reports that there were 175 different projects in MKULTRA. We know of only about a half-dozen. These were secret experiments with swine fever, dingy fever, deadly diseases, and psychedelic drugs on American and other population groups. In San Francisco and New York, for example, the CIA set up safe apartments and hired women who would lure men into them and slip them drinks containing LSD and other hallucinogenic drugs while hidden cameras recorded their reactions. When the experiment was over, the men were shoved back onto the street, unaware that they had been victims of drug experiments from which they might suffer long-term consequences. President Ford, if you recall, delivered a $1 million settlement to the widow of Dr. Carson, who had committed suicide after CIA pseudo-scientists had slipped him an LSD mickey.

Special light bulbs were placed in the Manhattan subways to disorient people and give them vertigo; the results were filmed at rush hour as the trains were whizzing past. Epidemics of whooping cough were triggered to see what would happen to a community if all the children had the disease—too bad about the weaker ones who might die in the process.

If you were reading the newspapers in October 1988, you noticed news of a settlement between the CIA and victims of similar experiments at McGill University in Canada, where the agency had been working with a psychiatrist who shot his patients up with hallucinogenic drugs—to experiment with their minds instead of healing them. Your tax dollars paid for the program and then paid damages to the victims. To date, not one CIA manager or pseudo-scientist has been put on trial, fired, disciplined, or even mildly reprimanded for MKULTRA activities.[18]

Inevitably, the question must be asked: Could AIDS be the accidental or intended result of one of the MKULTRA projects? The answer is that we will probably never know. The government is not about to open those macabre files for public scrutiny, exposing itself to thousands, if not millions, of lawsuits. But we do know that an anthrax experiment went so awry they had to seal part of a building at Fort Dietrich, Maryland from human entry for many years. The government has admitted that canisters of deadly microbes have been stolen from their laboratories.

Personally, I am skeptical that AIDS was deliberately concocted by anyone to target homosexuals and minorities. Nor does it seem to me that the government has deliberately ignored the AIDS problem. Rather, self-serving health authorities may have exploited the AIDS crisis, possibly inhibiting the broadest possible research and hence early discovery of the disease's real causes. In the mid-1980s, the National Institutes of Health and the former U.S. Surgeon General added to the hysteria and stigma surrounding the disease by insisting that AIDS, defined by testing positive to the HIV virus, was "100 percent fatal" and that millions would surely die in the near future.

AIDS is a dread disease that very likely will kill millions of people in the next 10-20 years. It is spreading from the population groups that were originally most devastated into the heterosexual community, rural areas, etc. Still, everyone who tests positive for HIV does not die, nor do unsafe sexual behaviors *automatically* transmit the disease, although the likelihood of transmission (of venereal diseases as well as HIV) is such that everyone should practice safe sex.

The current best evidence—the published guidelines to scientists and doctors working in AIDS research and treatment—is that a single exposure to HIV (for example, one incident of anal intercourse or an accidental puncture with a hypodermic needle that has previously been used on a person with AIDS) entails a one-in-two-hundred chance of AIDS infection. The figures currently being published by national medical authorities on the number of Americans testing positive for HIV, who will probably die in the next decade, and the number of Americans who have died of AIDS since 1980 (79,587, according to the Texas Department of Health, Bureau of Statistics) are almost certainly inaccurate.

My point is this: every person must take responsibility for practicing safe sex. But AIDS is also a "national security" issue, and we have solid grounds to mistrust our government officials on the subject of public health. The MKULTRA program was run by the CIA and the U.S. military with extensive help from doctors in prestigious institutions, like Harvard, Johns Hopkins, and McGill University medical schools. When Congress investigated MKULTRA in the early 1970s, it did not publish its detailed findings, which were classified for "national security reasons." It did not publish the details of the 170-odd projects that entailed experimentation with disease and drugs. It did not enact laws that would curtail such activity and protect the public from further experimentation.

In the alleged interests of national security, our leaders have been risking and sacrificing millions of people's lives in overt and covert wars, in the arms race, and in the areas of environmental and public health. The dead and the threatened should demand openness and accountability. The truth is vital both to national security and to the process of democracy.

Colonel George White, one of the founders of the MKULTRA program, also one of the OSS founders of the CIA, retired at about the time I joined the agency in the mid-1960s. He wrote a letter to a friend, subsequently published with his permission. According to White, "I toiled wholeheartedly in the vineyards because it was fun, fun, fun. Where else could a red-blooded American boy lie, kill, cheat, steal, rape and pillage with the blessings of the all highest?"[19]

MHCHAOS and COINTELPRO were CIA and FBI programs that began after World War II to manipulate, disrupt, and redirect student, labor, and civic organizations. In 1976, the Church Committee found that these programs were getting journalists— up to about 200 of them, including some of the biggest names in the business—to cooperate with the CIA and put its propaganda into our media so that we would be influenced by misrepresentations of what was happening in Southeast Asia, or Korea, or Vietnam, or China, or Central America, or other parts of the world that our government wanted to destabilize, attack, or where it wanted to fight a war.

THE CIA ON CAMPUS

From its very creation, actually beginning with its predecessor, the OSS during World War II, the CIA has coopted professors to manipulate student groups and to build files on students. It has published over 1,200 books, paying professors, scholars, and journalists to write and publish in their own names. These books are still in our libraries today because the Church Committee was not able to force the CIA to reveal the titles—the CIA protested that its "sources and methods," meaning the professors who had been writing CIA propaganda, would be revealed. The result is that if you are researching the Vietnam War, for example, or Cuba, or Nicaragua, a fair number of the books listed in your bibliography will be CIA propaganda pieces that deliberately misrepresent the facts.

This is not ancient history. At about the same time, in 1984, there was a flap at Harvard University when it was revealed that one of its professors had received $105,000 from the CIA for a book he was writing about the Middle East.

During the era of protest against the Vietnam War, CIA recruiters had to be very careful of any activity on university campuses. Certainly they didn't dare put overt recruiters on the campuses. Things had changed dramatically by the time Reagan was elected in 1980. During the 1980s, the CIA actually placed resident staffers on campuses under a formal program they hoped would achieve a status like the Army ROTC.

I have personally witnessed the effectiveness of this program. For a couple of years, I was invited to speak to the World Affairs Conference in Boulder, Colorado, by organizers who wanted to counterbalance the massive governmental representation there. So I went and did my duty sitting on panels and also standing in the audience to challenge the official representatives of the FBI, State Department, and CIA, who were making outrageous statements, grossly misrepresenting the facts of history, and essentially selling the interests of the secret government and the Reagan administration's program in Central America.

In one instance, a CIA representative, Mr. Bill Johnson, managed to get himself on the committee that formulated the conference's agenda, and then gained control of the committee that discussed the CIA on university campuses. Mr. Johnson carefully stacked the committee in his favor: it included two Canadians, one of whom made no effort to discuss the subject of the panel—namely the CIA on campus—but made broad patriotic statements in support of secrecy. The other Canadian was Peter Dale Scott of the University of California, Berkeley, who is an avid scholar of CIA history, but stated that he preferred not to get into the issue of the CIA on U.S. campuses. Scott then offered to turn his position on the panel over to me, noting that I had delivered 500 lectures on campuses across the nation, often debating the issue of the presence of CIA recruiters. Johnson adamantly refused to permit the switch, so when it was Scott's turn to speak, he yielded his time to me and I spoke from the audience.

I pointed out that Johnson was a retired 30-year CIA careerist (not a secret, but it had not been announced at the conference or published in its literature) who had been my boss in Vietnam in 1973.[20] Johnson was furious with my revelation; he wanted to have it both ways, i.e., to participate in academia but hide his CIA past from audiences as he manipulated panels for propaganda purposes. As a result of my revelation members of the organizing committees used insulting and abusive language to me over the phone and I was never invited back to the World Affairs Conference. The CIA, FBI, State Department, and CIA representatives, however, all returned to the conference year after year and continued their propagandistic activities virtually unchallenged.

Other than these sorts of forums, the CIA works the campuses from covert offices in its Foreign Resources Division, the euphemistic title for its *domestic* covert operations division. Case officers in this division work out of branch offices scattered about the nation [text deleted here by the CIA's Publications Review Board]. There are enough of them that they keep in touch with every major campus in the nation. They work with professors, using aliases on various programs. Their activities include building files on students whom the professors help them target.

For example, if there is a foreign student from a country the CIA is interested in, or a U.S. graduate student who is going to study in that country [text deleted here by the CIA's Publications Review Board]. Finally, when the student actually arrives in the country in question, the CIA will reveal itself and propose to continue the collaboration on a formal basis. At this point, the student must consider the potential for blackmail. Innocently stumbling into the CIA's web while studying in the U.S., his espionage may be revealed and his or her life wrecked if he or she does not cooperate.

There have been many thousands of such approaches over the years and the United States pays a price for them in the credibility of its legitimate business and academic institutions. The CIA places case officers overseas under every conceivable cover, thereby tainting real tourists, scholars, business people, even missionaries. The result is that people in countries throughout the world learn that, even though they would like to be friendly with a visiting American, it may not be safe or wise to invite them into their homes. For example, after I left the agency, I was lecturing at Michigan State University. The organizer of my visit was a Ph.D. candidate who had studied for three years in Zambia. As we drove about, she told me of another American scholar in Zambia who was "...well known to be CIA, I was warned about him almost from the day I arrived, so I avoided ever having anything to do with him for the three years I was in the country." Her story made me want to cry. As supervisor of CIA activities in Zambia during the time she was there, I was intimately familiar with every "asset" the CIA had in the country and the person she named was *not* one of them. Americans in Zambia mistrusted and avoided one another because the CIA had poisoned the environment. Frankly, my guess is that if Congress were investigating this aspect of CIA operations, they would find that most CIA managers actually *preferred* that other Americans in the country not trust one another.

The argument that is often given for the CIA's presence on campuses is that the First Amendment guarantees that everyone, including the CIA, have the opportunity to make their case directly. While this may seem overpowering, it is obviated by the CIA's massive covert activities on campuses. As long as the organization continues to subvert academia and to use it as a working field for covert manipulations and the generation and publication of propaganda, it cannot also claim the overt protections of the First Amendment.

But of course it does. In 1980, Harvard University attempted to pass an internal regulation that required professors to report any relationship they had with the CIA. Under orders from Director Admiral Stansfield Turner, the CIA sued Harvard, claiming a violation of the First Amendment, and won the right to continue its covert relationships and manipulations.

THE WAR AT HOME

The popular broom that is used by advocates of the system to sweep critics of the national security establishment aside is to brand them as "conspiratorialists" (a word an editor used in his letter rejecting this book). I was a "compulsive," he wrote. Anyone who is trying to penetrate the pablum that is generally taught in our schools and the party lines of the media to analyze how the system works can thus be brushed aside. (Other devices have been to label critics as "Communists," radicals, liberals, and even terrorists.) Oh, they disclaim, he believes it's all a great conspiracy!, as though politicians and their campaign staffs do not wrack their brains to devise ways to raise money (from special interest groups) to sell their agenda to the public, while covering their foibles and failings; as though President Reagan did not know that by focussing paranoid public attention on Nicaragua (the "Communist beach head in our own backyard!"), he was generating an atmosphere of support for his military spending; as though George Bush did not know in the fall of 1990 that he had been orchestrating public opinion behind a war in the Persian Gulf.)

How mindful is the orchestration of public opinion, of what Noam Chomsky calls "manufacturing consent?" Just reflect on one tiny item, namely the FBI's Library Analysis Program, which polls libraries across the nation to determine what people are reading.

In September 1988, FBI Director William Sessions announced that he was disciplining officers he found had been improperly targeting the Committee in Solidarity with the People of El Salvador (CISPES) and 160 other civic organizations, many of which were critical of the Reagan administration's policy in Central America. During the summer of 1989, committees of the Congress announced the finding that there were a total of 1,600 groups that had been targeted and listed, improperly, by the FBI. These programs were like the CIA's MHCHAOS and FBI's COINTELPRO programs, both of which had officially been dismantled. The CIA did the same thing during the 1980s, but there has been no confession or revelation of what they were doing. Nor did the committees publish a list of the names of the groups that had been targeted or listed by the FBI.

Some people, leaning over backwards to be fair, have tried to claim that to have an individual's or group's name listed doesn't hurt anything. In fact, it can lead to grievous consequences. The FBI cooperates with numerous other law enforcement organizations both within and outside the United States. For example, if you are an El Salvadoran refugee in this country and you attend a CISPES meeting and are then observed by the FBI and listed as a "terrorist," it can cost you your life if you are deported to El Salvador. It can also endanger your life if you are a U.S. citizen traveling abroad to a country like El Salvador and the FBI has listed you as a terrorist because of some association you've had, and shared that information with the death squads in San Salvador.

To cite a more specific example, in 1985, peace activist Brian Willson was registered by the FBI as a terrorist because of a non-violent fast he did on the steps of the U.S. Capitol in Washington. Later in 1985, he did a sit-in on the railroad tracks that carried shipments of ammunition from the Concord Naval Weapons Station in California. The FBI informed the station's security officers who advised the engineers of the train that some "known terrorists" were preparing to try to stop the train, in spite of the fact that Willson and the other protestors had abundantly advised the Navy and local civilian security officers of the utterly peaceful nature of their protest. They had also invited press coverage, again of their peaceful demonstration. The train engineers, however, were terrified at the thought of having their train seized by terrorists. Instead of stopping, they sped up the train and ran over Willson, cutting off his legs. Miraculously, he was not killed.

Organizations that are targeted and penetrated by secret federal agents are seriously disrupted. The public record is replete with exposés of agents encouraging illegal activity, including murder, to discredit the organization in question. Once members of an organization commit serious crimes, the Justice Department can pursue them in open court and the public sees them as criminals.

Less dramatically, domestic covert operations set people to fighting, disrupting their organizations from within. The so-called peace movement is notoriously fractious, and writhes in guilt at its inability to function peacefully. "Peaceniks" are among the most independent-minded people in the world, each with his or her own view of how things should be done and often emotionally volatile. Yet, at least some of the resulting dissension is fomented by professional agents in their midst. It takes only one intelligent, professionally trained provocateur to set a group to fighting until it disintegrates. The beauty of it from the government's point of view is that such groups have a horror of self-analysis, and its agents often go on from one group to the next making trouble.

I know personally how this works. In 1987, I put together a national association, called the Association for Responsible Dissent (ARDIS), that seemed to have tremendous energy. For the first year, its activities went swimmingly. Then a series of incidents occurred that defied logic. On occasion, members proposed activities that were irresponsible, reprehensible, and would have been illegal, had we not cut them off.

For example, although the organization was adamantly opposed to covert operations, one officer began to raise funds to finance an unrepentant mercenary killer to organize a *coup d'état* in Asia. Such fundraising is illegal. The officer also tried to implicate a prominent congressional committee in this plot, which could have grievously sabotaged the committee's effectiveness. Other officers proposed financial arrangements that our attorneys warned would have entailed fraud and conspiracy to defraud the government. Prominent members wrote poison-pen letters hinting at financial impropriety (after our books had been audited by two independent CPAs) and mailed the letters to potential funders, effectively killing any chance of our receiving any substantial grants.

Factions quickly formed until the group's principle expense seemed to be huge telephone bills as individuals gossiped, lobbied, and jockeyed for positions of leadership. In 1988, I was obliged to close the association down lest it lead to a major scandal. Among the many frustrations, shared by nearly all members, was doubt. We will never know if we were simply unable to get along, if some of our members merely had bad judgment, or if there was an agent or two in our midst fomenting the dissention.

At about the time I was closing the group down, FBI Director William Sessions announced his crackdown on illegal harassment of civic groups by federal agents, and the following summer the congressional committees followed up with their broader findings. Even in a "free society" like the United States, it would be too much to ask that we be given a list of the organizations that were targeted, so we could know what happened to our own.[21]

THE NEW LAWS

The British intelligence service worked during World War

II and afterwards to influence the United States to create its own secret service. It was British advisors who planted the idea that the CIA should have protection from public scrutiny, modeled on Britain's Official Secrets Act. Every CIA Director has lobbied and dreamed of such broad protection for the agency's activities. Because of the principles of our sacred Bill of Rights, accomplishing this has not been easy for the CIA, but it has nevertheless quietly made dramatic inroads into our civil liberties. A number of changes have been made through executive orders, legislation, and court rulings that protect CIA activities and crimes from prosecution. These laws often operate at the direct expense of individual freedoms.

For example:

- In *United States v. Victor Marchetti,* the Supreme Court granted the CIA the right to pre-publication censorship of book manuscripts.
- In *CIA v. Harvard,* the CIA challenged a university regulation that required any professors who had private arrangements with the CIA to report them to the university president. The CIA won. It was ruled that such a regulation violated the CIA's and the professors' freedom of speech. Consequently, the CIA can continue to maintain secret agent relationships with professors and covertly manipulate research or student activities without the knowledge of the university.
- In *United States v. Frank Snepp,* the CIA successfully sued Snepp for damages and was awarded the profits from his book, *Decent Interval,* on the grounds that he had violated his fiduciary responsibility and the secrecy agreements he had signed with the agency promising to submit any writings for review.
- In my own case, the agency was able to seize the profits from my first book, *In Search of Enemies,* under the Supreme Court's Snepp ruling.
- In *United States v. Philip Agee,* the State Department was able to obtain the right to withdraw a citizen's passport without citing any suspected criminal misconduct as grounds. This ruling asserts, as a matter of

principle, that the United States can deny citizens the right to travel freely.

- In *United States v. Progressive Magazine,* the government attempted to prohibit publication of an article about the fabrication of atomic weapons that was based on information available in the public library. They were, happily, not successful.

- In the Truong Humphries criminal prosecution, the CIA obtained a 15-year sentence for Mr. Humphries' passage of some lowly classified documents to the Vietnamese in his efforts to get his family out of Vietnam. President Jimmy Carter took a personal interest in this case, virtually ordering its prosecution when there were other options available. Some would consider this to be an abuse of presidential influence, if not power, in the exaggerated interests of national security.

- In 1982, the Official Identities Protection Act was passed, making it a felony to identify secret agents even if, for example, they have penetrated your own civic group and are willfully disrupting it.

- In 1984, Secretary of State George Shultz lobbied vigorously for the passage of a Preemptive Strikes Bill that would permit the Secretary of State to formulate a list of "suspected terrorists." The government would then have legal immunity if it kicked in the door of people on that list and killed them, striking preemptively against their suspected terrorism. The proposed bill prohibited anyone whose name was on the list from going to court and suing to have their name removed. While lobbying for this bill, Shultz publicly admitted that violent actions would be undertaken against people on the basis of information that would never stand up in a court of law and that innocent people would be hurt in the process. Even the *New York Times,* which supports many, but not all, of the CIA's rights to secrecy, protested the Preemptive Strikes Bill, noting that it was identical to Hitler's "Night and Fog" program. Congress refused to pass the original bill. So the government quietly implemented the sinister program without legislation!

As noted above, "listing" an individual in FBI or police files can have hideous consequences for the victim. First, he or she doesn't know they are listed. Just consider the treatment they will receive in jail if they are arrested—innocent or guilty— and routine checks indicate he or she is a "terrorist." Or, again, a Salvadoran visitor to the U.S. who attends a meeting, is photographed by the FBI and registered as a "known terrorist," and then returns or is forcibly sent home may face death the moment he steps off the plane.

Or consider the treatment any citizen can expect in jail when arrested—innocent or guilty—and routine police checks indicate that he or she is a "terrorist."

- Verne Lyon was recruited to work for the CIA on the Iowa State campus and subsequently implicated in the criminal activities of a group the agency was targeting. He was blackmailed into going under deep cover in Cuba for the agency. Eventually, the Cubans expelled him from their country. The FBI hounded him out of Canada and then kidnapped him off the streets of Peru and flew him back to the United States to stand trial. Obviously, Lyon endeavored to obtain his CIA file to prove he had been a government agent when the crime had taken place. The CIA's general counsel flew to Kansas City to confer with the judge who then took it upon himself to manage the trial as necessary to protect the "national security." Lyon was denied access to his CIA files. He was convicted and sentenced to 17 years in Leavenworth. On appeal, he won the right to a retrial, but the same judge, citing "national security," insisted on retrying the case. Lyon was once again convicted and sentenced to 17 years. He served six before he was released on parole.

- Ronald Rewold was caught in a CIA S & L-type scandal in Hawaii. The CIA was so desperate to make sure its role in the scandal did not come out that its general counsel moved to Hawaii and took a position as assistant district attorney, personally trying the case. The judge sternly forbade the defense attorneys from making this information known to the jury. Without question, it would have influenced their decision.

However, in a reverse manipulation of the law, in order to protect CIA operatives in the Iran/*contra* scandal, charges were dropped against several obviously guilty officers because the protection of national security secrets would allegedly prevent their fair trial.

- In the famous case of John Walker and family, the government made a convincing case during the trial that the Walkers had delivered sensitive information to agents of the Soviet Union. The prosecution asserted that the "enemy" already had the information because of the Walkers' treason, and the trial was public. Nevertheless CIA Director William Casey threatened NBC television, The *Washington Post,* and the journalist Seymour Hersh with prosecution if they reported the details of the trial.

- During the invasion of Grenada in 1983, the press was physically restricted from the island during the operation. Hence all the information available to the public about the action was tailored by the U.S. Army PSYWAR propagandists. When the dust settled a compromise was worked out by the General Seidel Commission, providing that in future invasions a press pool would accompany the landing force and be able to transmit edited stories through the commander's communications network. This arrangement was tested during National Guard training exercises in Honduras and is in effect today in the military buildup of U.S. forces in Saudi Arabia.

- President Reagan's controversial Attorney General, Edwin Meese III, and occasionally Reagan himself, disparaged the Constitution as "only a piece of paper" that could and should be discounted. Although they did not succeed in abolishing this sacred document, they apparently made secret provisions to do so. It is now well documented that during the Reagan administration, the

Federal Emergency Management Agency (FEMA) established procedures and prepared facilities for the declaration of martial law during national emergencies. A total of ten military bases were prepared to receive 400,000 possible aliens and dissidents in a time of crisis or controversy like the Vietnam War. During the Iran/-contra joint congressional hearings of 1987, the Miami Herald published an article reporting that FEMA's plans included the suspension of the Constitution. When this article was mentioned during the Iran/contra hearings by Representative Jack Brookes, the committee chair, Senator Daniel Inouye admonished him that the question involved secret information and could not be discussed publicly.

Note the implications: the national security complex has secret plans to suspend the Constitution without due process or consultation of the people whom that Constitution supposedly protects.

All across the country, states, cities, and counties were simultaneously encouraged to formulate local ordinances that could be used to control the population in a time of discord. Often such ordinances are well camouflaged. For example, during the Democratic national convention in San Francisco in 1984, the renowned anti-nuclear Livermore Action Group organized an imaginative bus tour of the multinational corporations' headquarters in the city and an entire busload was arrested on the felony charge of "obstructing a sidewalk." Obviously bus tours are normal all over the country, and charges were not pressed. However all of those activists were placed on notice during the week of the convention that they could be prosecuted if they were picked up for any other protest activity.

Meanwhile President Reagan gleefully stacked the federal court system with conservative judges that, he was assured, would enforce the new laws whenever called upon to do so. He boasted as he left office that 45 percent of the sitting judges were his appointees.

And now, the War on Drugs has provided a better justification than anti-Communism ever did for curtailing individual freedoms. People who are suspected of running drugs can see their property confiscated without due process of the law. Their bank accounts can be frozen before they are tried so they are unable to hire attorneys for their defense.

Such is the cynicism of the national security establishment in curtailing individual freedoms.

THE DRUG WAR: A CLOSER LOOK

"The first casualty when war comes is the truth," observed Senator Hiram Johnson in 1917, three years after the United States launched its goal of a "drug-free" America. The axiom is as true of the Drug War as any other. The "drug problem" in U.S. society, while serious, is being distorted for ominous political purpose and to justify draconian legal processes.

Staunch conservative commentators are now joining liberals in acknowledging that the damage being done to U.S. society by the Drug War is measurably greater than the drug problem itself. Even former Secretary of State George Shultz, who supported the bombing of Tripoli in April 1986, advocates some form of legalization of what are now "controlled substances." Sane columnists and commentators ranging from Anthony Lewis to Ted Koppel and William F. Buckley Jr. are expressing their concern.[22] After some years of political bombast and war-like propaganda, the truth about the Drug War is catching up with the rhetoric in dozens of books, articles, essays, columns, and television documentaries.

The current War on Drugs, with its broad rationales for aggressive response, police action, and stringent new laws, has quickly replaced the old anti-Christ of Communism in the hearts and minds of the national security establishment. This War on Drugs, complete with body-counts, noble posturing against sin, and continual government duplicity, is a means for politicians to assure the public that they are "doing something" about the drug problem. The drug problem they are addressing is monumentally distorted and exaggerated. It is political bread-and-circuses, which is being used to effect draconian changes in the U.S. judicial process at the expense of individual liberties while diverting our attention from the nation's more pressing problems: a crushing $4 trillion debt, a dying planet, urban decay, deteriorating infrastructure, higher taxes for average U.S. citizens, all of which add up to declining standards of living and quality of life for most of us.

Drugs of all kinds are a serious problem in the modern world. People are killed and lives are wrecked by drugs. In 1985, according to figures published by the U.S. Bureau on Mortality and the National Institute on Drug Abuse, 3,562 people died as a direct result of "drug" (controlled substances, hereafter: CS-drugs) use, not one of them from marijuana. This is about the same as the number of people the EPA estimates died of passive smoking. During that same year, about 7,000 people died of overdoses of prescription drugs, over one million died from smoking, alcohol, and dietary—fatty foods—abuse. And yet, under the auspices of the Drug War, a Drug Czar has been appointed to wage a war on CS-drugs. The military has become directly involved in policing U.S. society and due process of law, including the principle of "innocent until proven guilty," is being abandoned. These changes are occurring while our taxes subsidize the cultivation of tobacco.

Under the new CS-drug laws, federal agents can confiscate your home, car, and even the funds with which you would hire an attorney to defend yourself, *without convicting you, indicting you, or even formally accusing you of a crime.* Consider the case of Bruce Lavoie, a machinist in Hudson, New Hampshire. Without announcing themselves and without evidence that Lavoie might be armed, the police broke through the door of his home with a battering ram and killed him while his son watched. They had a warrant based in part on a 20-month-old informant's tip, and found a single marijuana cigarette. Or consider the owner of the Detroit food market who was held and his receipts seized after dogs sniffed cocaine on three one dollar bills in his cash register.

Innocent until proven guilty? Again, all this can be done without a conviction, without even an indictment or formal accusation of criminal activity.

Harper's editor, Lewis Lapham, writes, "The war on drugs is a folly and a menace.... The drug war, like all wars, sells papers, and the media, like the politicians, ask for nothing better than a safe and profitable menace. The campaign against drugs involves most of the theatrical devices employed by "Miami

Vice": scenes of crime in progress (almost always dressed up, for salacious effect, with the cameo appearance of one or two prostitutes), melodramatic villains in the Andes, a vocabulary lifted from a Tom Clancy novel, and the specter of a crazed lumpenproletariat rising in revolt in the nation's cities."

The federal agents of the Drug War are *not* pursuing other murderers (who kill 23,000 per year), rapists, and car thieves. But the Drug War is losing its political steam. Even William Bennett, the original U.S. "drug czar" has returned to private life to seek more viable issues with which to build his career. However, there is an important axiom to keep in mind, namely that people in power are traditionally reluctant to relinquish whatever controlling laws they have managed to implement. This is to say that the damage to the Bill of Rights that has been effected in the name of the Drug War will be permanent unless deliberate steps are taken to restore the sacred liberties.

Who profits from our present drug laws and war? The massive bureaucracy devoted to fighting the War on Drugs as well as the drug czars in Colombia and other, less publicized, parts of the world. Our current policies deliver to the criminal czars a *drug tariff* of about $100 billion per year, capital which they can use to bribe and corrupt our legal system. The price of cocaine is inflated 40 times by our laws, fueling the criminal mayhem that besets us.

We cannot forget the Senate's Kerry Committee findings of: cocaine smuggling on CIA/*contra* aircraft; reports on the number of prosecutions in which the CIA has intervened to block prosecution of drug smugglers; the drug-dealing creep Manuel Noriega's twenty-odd year relationship with the CIA (before they had a falling-out).

In the mindless passion of war, we have outlawed the growth of hemp, forgetting that for 200 years it was extremely valuable for rope, fabric, paper, and fuel—hence all the Hemphills and Hempsteads across the land. In World War II the U.S. government even went so far as to produce a film, *Hemp for Victory*. Hemp farmers and their sons were exempted from military service, so valuable was the fiber in dozens of applications ranging from fire hoses to the life preserver that saved young George Bush's life when his plane crashed in the Pacific.

The remarkable hemp plant offers dramatic but taboo solutions to fuel shortages and to the "greenhouse effect." One acre of growing hemp equals 4 1/2 acres of forest in oxygen exchange, while petroleum fuel obviously returns no oxygen to the air. (Note: I personally do not smoke the mood-altering hemp flower; neither, however, do I inhale brain-damaging gasoline or glue fumes. But I do note that we do not outlaw gasoline because its fumes are deadly when sniffed.) Grown on 7 percent of U.S. land, hemp could provide all 75 quadrillion billion BTUs the U.S. uses annually, rendering Saddam Hussein and the Saudis irrelevant to our lives and economic problems.

The cynicism of the War on Drugs is measurable as well in the historical record of the CIA itself, and other branches of the U.S. government, including the White House and Justice Department under President Reagan, which have been at least indirectly involved with the protection of drug dealers. The Drug Enforcement Agency itself has published the fact that, in the 1970s, before the cocaine boom of the 1980s, the CIA had intervened in 27 cases to block the prosecutions of drug smugglers and dealers.

Over the decades, every major catastrophic area in which the CIA has worked has left behind a major functioning drug cartel. The "French Connection" grew directly from the OSS, the CIA's predecessor, which got "Lucky" Luciano out of prison during World War II and paid him to activate the Mafia to work with U.S. security agencies, initially on the nation's docks in East Coast ports, where they feared sabotage. Eventually, he and other Mafia contacts were recruited to assist the Allies in Italy and southern France where, needless to say, they continued their criminal activities. Immediately after the war, they were intensely active in Germany, trading in munitions, drugs, and penicillin, not to mention trying to get their hands on some of the $2 billion (at 1980 values) in gold that disappeared from the Reichsbank. Soon the CIA was hiring them to violently intimidate strikers on the docks in southern France. Their drug activities quickly grew into the pipeline from the Middle East that became known as the French Connection. Luciano moved to

Cuba to establish a link between this pipeline and the United States.

The "Golden Triangle" in Southeast Asia also grew directly out of the CIA's covert activities there. Previously, the opium trade had been dominated by French Intelligence with the Corsican Mafia. The CIA took over, with its Air America and Civil Air Transport aircraft flying arms to its drug-smuggling allies and flying back out with the heroin. The first market was U.S. GI's during the Vietnam War and the second was the United States itself.

The "Golden Crescent" in Afghanistan is allegedly the largest covert operation the CIA has run to date in terms of money spent, although it has not been particularly controversial. Begun under President Carter and CIA Director Stansfield Turner, it cost many hundreds of million of dollars during the 1980s, with CIA air transports hauling arms and, inevitably, drugs. During the first five years of its implementation, the region's Golden Crescent grew into the world's largest source of heroin.

During about the same period of time the CIA implemented another major destabilization program in Central America, in which it had numerous aircraft flying continuously into and out of every country, to and from the United States, and through islands in the Caribbean. It can be no surprise that during this same period of time the Medellin cocaine cartel became a multibillion dollar industry. The importation of cocaine into the United States in 1981, according to figures published by the Drug Enforcement Agency, was 12,000-17,000 kilograms. By 1987, it had jumped to an estimated 70,000-100,000 kilograms, a little over 100 tons.

The public record includes numerous instances in which people related to the CIA's *contra* program were involved in smuggling cocaine. Several court cases turned up evidence of involvement by *contras* and CIA subsidiary companies that were supporting the *contras'* involvement in drug smuggling. The Senate Committee headed by John Kerry (D-MA) estimated that 50-100 flights of CIA/*contra* aircraft had hauled cocaine and marijuana back into the United States. Milian Rodriguez presented testimony and documents at his trial that several million dollars in cash had been paid by the Medellin cartel to the *contras,* buying access to the aircraft pipeline into the United States. Felix Rodriguez, a long-time CIA agent who had landed in the Bay of Pigs a few days before the CIA's ill-fated landing in 1961 and served in Military Region III in Vietnam with the CIA chief of base, Don Gregg (later Vice-President George Bush's national security advisor), was in charge of the *contra* air effort working out of Ilopango in El Salvador. Rodriguez was also named as having been involved in receiving money for the *contras* from the Medellin cartel.

Federal attorneys in Florida reported that they received instructions from the Justice Department in Washington, apparently originating with Attorney General Ed Meese, obstructing their prosecutions of drug smugglers on the grounds of "national security." Other law enforcement officers in the DEA, Customs, and the FBI had similar experiences. Lt. Col. Oliver North's files specifically mentioned $14 million in drug money being used in the *contra* program. (Remember that he spent three days shredding his more sensitive files.)

The beauty of the *contra* program for the Medellin cartel was that the people running the program from the CIA and the White House were either indulgent and/or eminently corruptible, while the airplanes that flew the arms down to Central America came back to land at National Guard and Air Force bases in the United States where the CIA had *de facto* immunity from security checks and regular customs and immigrations inspections.[23]

THE KENNEDY ASSASSINATION

For many years now, when people in this country have been polled with the question, "Do you believe that Lee Harvey Oswald acted alone in killing John Kennedy, or was there a conspiracy?" 80 percent of them respond that they believe there was a conspiracy. But they often back off when pressed to guess what form the conspiracy actually took. Lee Harvey Oswald, the accused assassin, probably had help in killing Kennedy, most people think. In fact, the House Assassination Committee concluded in 1979 that there *was* a conspiracy to kill President Kennedy but, incredibly, the Justice Department did not respond with an investigation. To repeat, our president was gunned down in broad daylight in what was almost certainly a conspiracy, and the Justice Department never undertook a criminal investigation to identify the conspirators!

By the spring of 1963, the liberal president John Kennedy had antagonized a number of powerful and very ugly forces in this country. The CIA's OPMONGOOSE/JMWAVE group, comprised of Cuban exiles and based on the University of Miami campus, was armed and trained in military-style ambushes. They had been attacking Cuba, like precursors of the Nicaraguan *contras,* destroying crops, brutalizing citizens, destabilizing the society, and conspiring with the Mafia to assassinate Fidel Castro and other leaders. From its CIA leaders down to the rank and file of Cuban exiles, the group's members hated Kennedy because of the Bay of Pigs fiasco. Although it was their own fault the 1961 landing had been bungled, they blamed Kennedy for not sending in the Marines to bail them out. And they hated him for finally resolving the Cuban missile crisis by making a deal with Soviet leader Nikita Khrushchev to have the Soviet missiles withdrawn from Cuba in exchange for a promise that the United States would not invade Cuba. There was also an important piece of disinformation, widely accepted by the OPMONGOOSE/JMWAVE fighters, that Kennedy had agreed that some Soviet missiles would remain behind in Cuba. In other words, many had convinced themselves that Kennedy was a traitor!

Further, in the summer of 1963, Kennedy had platoons of Customs officers raiding the exiles' camps and shutting them down, and he had extended tentative feelers toward Fidel Castro for possible normalization of relations.

The right-wing military was angry because Kennedy had decided to pull U.S. military advisors out of the Vietnam War. Conservative Dallas businessmen were angry because he was moving to terminate the oil depletion allowances that had made them so wealthy over a period of years. The Deep South was becoming enraged because he was beginning a (very tentative) program to stop segregation.

The Mafia was embattled. John Kennedy, the President, and his brother Bobby, the Attorney General, had for years been waging a war against the Mafia, trying to put its leaders in jail, throwing Carlos Marcello, the *don* from New Orleans, out of the country, and going after the organization in a serious, systematic way. It turned out that there were numerous threats and other indications of the Mafia's plans to kill the Kennedy brothers. It was, as the Mafia saw it, part of a war.

By mid-1963, in fits of rage, John Birchers, Klansmen, Minutemen, and rabid radicals were running ads in newspapers calling the President a traitor. At least a half dozen plots against the President's life were known to be hatching, but the FBI was firmly in the grasp of the megalomaniac J. Edgar Hoover, who resented the Kennedys. J. Edgar Hoover was a master of blackmail and everyone in Washington knew it. He kept files on Senators and Congresspeople; his agents worked diligently to accumulate dirt on every important person in Washington. If anyone dared to cross Hoover, exposure was the result. If anyone tried to force an investigation of the FBI, exposure was the result. If anyone tried to force serious investigations of the Mafia, exposure would result.

The President was perfunctorily warned of the threats against him, but the usual vigilant efforts to protect him were not taken. The Secret Service, FBI, and local police certainly *can* protect presidents. They do it continuously not only inside the United States but in foreign capitals around the world. Numerous, almost routine, techniques are involved, like bringing extra security forces to blanket problem areas, moving in caravans of cars at a brisk 45 miles an hour, and using, whenever possible, unannounced routes that do not include sharp, slow turns.

When President Kennedy and his wife visited Dallas on November 22, 1963, nearly all of the protections were lifted. Available Texas Guard units were not called into the city and available Dallas policemen were temporarily released from duty. The result? A team of CIA, Cuban exile, and Mafia-related renegades organized a simple military ambush in Dallas and successfully gunned him down. The ambush and its coverup were brazen and astonishingly open. In fact several plots, in Chicago, Miami, and Houston, to kill Kennedy had misfired or been thwarted. The plot that succeeded in Dealey Plaza was so open that various people were reported prior to the event to have said that Kennedy would be killed with a rifle and a patsy would be blamed for the crime. Individuals like Joseph Milteer, the "umbrella man," and a CIA pilot Robert Plumlee went to Dealey Plaza on the 22nd of November to watch.

Obviously, most CIA personnel were not involved and did not know of the plot since sensitive operations are compartmentalized in order to protect their security. Moreover, the great majority of the coat-and-tie people inside CIA headquarters would never have put up with a hit on the President. A great deal of the success of the CIA is due to its ability to attract patriotic, good soldiers who believe in the general rightness of what they do, and then insulate them through compartmentalization from the heavier activities.

The OPMONGOOSE renegades, however, included assassins, terrorists, and people who had been involved in the drug traffic from Cuba into the United States. The team set up a military-style ambush in Dealey Plaza, with shooters on the tops of buildings and the famous grassy knoll. The route of the President's convoy included a 120-degree turn which slowed the car to a near stop. There was cooperation of elements of the Secret Service, of the Dallas Police, and of other law enforcement agencies.

When the shooting began, the Secret Service driver put on the brakes (home movies of the scene show the brake lights on).

Anyone who has been through that kind of training—and I have been through their "bang and burn" courses—is drilled to react. When the bullets start flying in such a situation, you mash down on the gas and you get the hell out of the area; you do not slow down and look around as the seasoned Secret Service driver in fact did. In ten seconds of rifle fire, only one of the Secret Service agents in the trail car moved to the President's aid. The one agent who did move was Jackie Kennedy's personal guard, in Dallas at her request, not part of the team that was there to protect the President.

Kennedy was shot at very close range from firing stations, probably four of them, where the assassins fired eight to ten shots. He was hit in the back, throat, and twice in the head, two bullets each from the front and from the back. Texas Governor John Connally was hit twice. Two bullets were fired into the concrete, one on each side of the convoy. After the shooting stopped, the convoy raced away. The FBI and other branches of the government immediately launched the coverup. The new President, Lyndon Johnson, ordered the limousine in which Kennedy was killed be flown to Chicago and destroyed. The announced goal of President Johnson was to "reassure" the nation by proving that the killing was the work of lone assassin Lee Harvey Oswald. It was variously suggested that an investigation that turned up Soviet involvement might lead to nuclear war; it might embarrass the Kennedy widow; it might lead to domestic unrest. In fact; it might have led to a sizeable number of very important people and organizations being implicated in a presidential assassination. That might very well have exercised the population sufficiently to provoke a serious investigation of CIA, FBI, and Mafia activities in the country, and to demand some changes.

The evidence was extensively tampered with. The President's body was altered; the photographs of the autopsy were altered; and over 100 witnesses were killed or died mysterious and violent deaths. To this day, despite the House Committee's 1979 conclusion that there was a conspiracy, there has been no formal, official investigation. Neither have all the documents been released.

Even among the majority that acknowledge that there was a broad conspiracy, many find it difficult to believe that the CIA itself could have been involved. Perhaps, they reluctantly concede, "renegades" might have had something to do with it.

In fact, there is strong evidence that both the FBI and the CIA high commands had prior knowledge of and direct involvement in the conspiracy. After the Dallas Police had arrested Lee Harvey Oswald, but before they could have positively identified him (he had false identification papers in his wallet) much less interrogate him and reasonably confirm his (alleged) guilt, FBI Director J. Edgar Hoover telephoned Bobby Kennedy in Washington to tell him that the assassin had been caught. Hoover gave Kennedy biographic information that he could only have had prior to the assassination. Clearly he was waiting with information about Lee Harvey Oswald, to blame him for the killing.

Similarly, CIA operatives far from Dallas were waiting with biographic information about Oswald to feed to the media. Some time after the Warren Committee hearings, journalist Seth Kantor found himself broadly suspected of being somehow a secret agent because, researchers found, the Warren Commission had classified part of his testimony. Puzzled, he checked and found that the Commission had in fact classified telephone calls he made during the afternoon of the killing. In addition to checking his own notes, he succeeded in forcing the Warren Commission to return his testimony to him, and identified the calls. One was to the managing editor of the Scripps-Howard news service bureau in Washington. Mid-afternoon, again long before the police could have interrogated Oswald, made a positive identification, concluded what had happened, and eliminated the possibility of accomplices in a conspiracy to kill the President, the editor told Kantor that Oswald had been identified as the assassin and instructed him to call Hal Hendricks, a journalist who gave Kantor detailed biographic information about Oswald. Years later, in the CIA-engineered coup in Chile, Hendricks was positively identified as a CIA operative working under journalistic cover. Moreover, the Warren Commission's move to classify the phone calls is proof positive that it knew there was an intelligence connection with Hendricks and strongly suggests that it was willfully covering up the assassination conspiracy.

In sum, the FBI Director and CIA media operatives were waiting, primed, before the assassination to launch the coverup and pin the blame on the pre-selected patsy, Oswald.

We have less hard evidence, but I personally believe from my knowledge of the CIA that elements of the CIA's ZRRIFLE program were probably involved in the conspiracy, along with Cuban exiles, and Sam Giancana, John Roselli, and Charles Nicoletti of organized crime. ZRRIFLE was exposed by the Senate Church Committee. The CIA's chief of operations, Richard Bissell, admitted to its existence as did its founder, a rough impetuous man named William Harvey, who boasted of his criminal connections. The committee obtained and published the CIA's project outline, which is the key document, setting up funding of any new project. For ZRRIFLE, Harvey wrote the outline in longhand so no secretary would read it. That document, and their testimony, confirm the existence of a formal assassination team that was managed by Harvey from the Cuba Desk inside the CIA's Langley headquarters and from the JMWAVE station on the University of Miami campus in Florida. It would be totally inconsistent with Allen Dulles' leadership of the CIA, its nature, and all its usage and operating procedures, for this unit, with all its political liabilities, to have been formed without Dulles' approval.

At the same time, CIA Director Richard Helms' admitted that he had approached organized crime through Bob Maheu, who was associated with Howard Hughes. Maheu made the introduction to Sam Giancana, a bloody-handed killer of the Chicago mob. The CIA put up $1 million (of course this would not include the overhead costs for the CIA's Florida operations) for the assassination of Fidel Castro. John Roselli was so deeply involved that, according to members of the JMWAVE station, he was in the offices so much that he was called "Colonel Roselli" and the staff thought he was a CIA officer instead of a Mafioso.

Harvey, who is described in David Martin's book, *Wilderness of Mirrors*(Harper & Row, 1980), may have been the ultimate "rogue elephant." During the Cuban missile crisis, when

President Kennedy and Nikita Khrushchev were running a bluff of historical dimensions that had the world teetering on the brink of nuclear war, William Harvey raced to jam teams from the OPMONGOOSE secret army into Cuba in anticipation of an invasion. In the volatile dynamics of the situation, the U.S. had told the Soviets that any effort to "blind" the U.S. by shooting down its U-2 reconnaissance planes would be taken as an act of war. The Soviets understood, but Fidel Castro personally controlled the ground-to-air missiles that could shoot the planes down, and he was enraged by the OPMONGOOSE team's violent activities. When everything had calmed down, Bobby Kennedy disciplined Harvey by exiling him to the Rome station where, ironically, he would be closer to the heart of Mafia leaders. This was a few months before John Kennedy was shot in Dallas.

This complex of violent, angry CIA, Cuban exile, and Mafia killers—all of them with deep, desperate grievances against the Kennedy brothers—almost certainly produced the team of about twelve men who set up the ambush in Dealey Plaza and fired the eight to ten shots that killed President Kennedy and wounded Governor Connally.

The Kennedy assassination was nothing less than a *coup d'état*. The elements involved, who hated the popular liberal John Kennedy, were faced with his re-election and possibly his brother's after that. They had been condoning, approving, and running *coups d'états*, assassinations, and programs of mayhem around the world. They could not be bothered to wait for democracy to take its course, so they plotted an ambush and they killed him. Kennedy's successor, Vice-President Lyndon Johnson, was a team man who played ball with all their interests, a politician who accepted money from the Mafia and was notorious for conducting dirty campaigns. After Johnson moved into the presidency, the plotters got everything they wanted, including the oil depletion allowance and the Vietnam War. The crusade against organized crime was dropped, and the world went on as they wanted it to, according to their wishes, without their having to bother with an election. Five years later, in 1968, the night he won the California primary which clinched the Democratic Party's presidential nomination, John

Kennedy's brother, Robert Kennedy, was also assassinated.[24]

THE PRAETORIAN GUARD

The arms race is wrecking the economies of both of the superpowers. To put it another way, although the Soviets have capitulated and largely renounced their Stalinist system, the United States has also lost the Cold War. Our national debt is now $4 trillion, and is double-compounding under interest payments and continuing trade deficits. By the year 2001, it will pass $10 trillion. The so-called "defense" corporations are multinational conglomerates that have no great loyalty to the United States; they are in fact no longer U.S. corporations but transnational entities loyal only to themselves. They make enormous profits and invest the money overseas. They are quite willing to sell the U.S. economy down the drain in order to continue making exaggerated profits. Doubts about the cynicism that big business and international financiers hold toward petty nationalism should have been dispelled long ago when major U.S. corporations dealt profitably with Hitler's Germany throughout World War II. Standard Oil sold petroleum to Germany in greater quantities and at lower prices than to the United States. ITT's German plants built the aircraft that strafed and bombed our soldiers during the Omaha Beach landing at Normandy. Well before the war, financiers met and created the Bank of International Settlements in Berne, Switzerland, which handled accounts and exchanges for and between both sides throughout the war. This is the bank in which the Germans deposited the $40 million in gold that they looted from the Czechoslovakian treasury and took from the bodies of victims in death camps, but it remained the bank of record for the U.S. Federal Reserve throughout the war.[25]

The United States is producing MX missiles, which are put in the ground where they can never be used except in the event of nuclear war. When a weapon is completed, it no longer produces jobs for U.S. workers. The factory that produced it must close down, or produce another one. Such weapons can never be traded to countries overseas. Meanwhile our allies— not our enemies—are producing VCRs and cars and passing us by with favorable trade balances, while we, the self-appointed policemen of the world, plunge deep into debt. While President Reagan was spending so much time promoting his *contra* program in Nicaragua, a country with two elevators, the Japanese succeeded in capturing 30 percent of the world's international overseas exchange and the United States became a debtor nation for the first time since before World War I, with the greatest debt in the history of the world.

It is more than ironic that the losers of World War II, Japan and Germany, won the Cold War precisely because they were prohibited from producing arms while the two bigger winners, pulsing with the testosterone poison of victory, plunged into world rivalry and dragged themselves both into secondary economic status.

The aftermath of the Cold War has left the United States military complex with empty rationales for its domination of U.S. society. The great Communist anti-Christ collapsed and the Soviet President was soon a "personal friend" of the U.S. President. The Pentagon quickly shifted emphasis to other "threats to the U.S. national security," like the War on Drugs and predicted crises in the Third World. Long ago, strategists of the military complex saw these changes coming. For years, Henry Kissinger has been observing that the United States and the Soviet Union had more in common with each other than either did with countries of the Third World. In 1945, immediately after World War II, George Kennan predicted that world conflict would eventually devolve into a conflict between the Haves of the northern industrial countries and the Have Nots of the southern hemisphere. Under President Jimmy Carter, in the 1970s, the United States began to develop and "sell" to the public a Rapid Deployment Force and capability in the U.S. military to respond to military crises in the Third World.

Note the immediate response of the military establishment to the Middle East crisis of August 1990. Following the end of the Cold War, the capitulation of Communism, the dismantling of the Berlin Wall, the U.S. military faced substantial cuts. Beginning with the B-2 Stealth bomber, the military establishment quickly seized upon the Iraqi invasion to restore threatened programs, their full budget, and their renewed influence in American society. Defense planners quickly began outlining their "needs" for new generations of tanks and aircraft and high-speed ships to deliver those tanks to Third World countries where future wars will be fought.

Nuclear weapons are relatively economical when compared to the costs of conventional armies and weapons. However, the military complex wants everything it can get. Pointing to the Middle East crisis, George Bush has expressed an urgent "need" for billions of dollars to advance Star Wars, the B-2 bomber, and buy Midgetman missiles.

The result of a runaway arms race is the production of arms. We have saturated the world—"booby-trapped it," as Carl Sagan says—with 60,000 thermonuclear weapons. In 1981, we had the capability to utterly destroy 80 Soviet Unions, to render 20 planets uninhabitable. Now, despite the INF Treaty, the world is far more dangerous than it was in 1981. The United States and the Soviet Union have effected a 40 percent increase in the numbers of their strategic weapons, and they have made them more modern and more efficient.

The United States is still racing to deploy the B-1b bomber, the B-2 Stealth bomber, the MX missile, the Trident II missiles, and, again, the Star Wars program. Meanwhile, the Soviet Union is continuing to deploy more accurate and more sophisticated strategic weapons that can target any corner of the United States. The Soviet Union, home of the Chernobyl plant, is now marketing a nuclear reactor for use in space. Any country that wants to buy one can. And there are nine other countries rushing to join the nuclear club.

THE PRAETORIAN GUARD: AT WORK IN THE PERSIAN GULF

In the early 1980s, I noted that either of the superpowers that eschewed the Cold War would not only *not* suffer dire consequences but would enjoy a walkover in terms of world opinion. In 1982, I published my second book, *Red Sunset,* in which I previewed *glasnost* by depicting a Russian who felt that peace instead of conflict would be a better course for the world. Sure enough, about three years later, Mikhail Gorbachev burst onto the world scene, determined to restructure at least the Soviet side of things. He has systematically dismantled the Soviet Bloc, even opening the Soviet Union itself to pluralism of political parties, and has enjoyed the world response that I predicted. Unfortunately, the West has been left in a bit of a quandary. While our leaders openly express their pleasure over "winning" the Cold War, there is also a muted sense of confusion. How can the system that is built on "enemies" function without them? If the United States won the Cold War, how come the world is cheering the other side? The American Way has prevailed, but the United States is no longer in control of its own economic destiny.

If the Cold War is over, as the leaders of both sides claim, and Communism is passé, then it follows that we hardly need the CIA, or at least its covert operations side. Right? So why does the CIA currently enjoy its largest budget ever? Why has the CIA's charter been officially expanded for the first time in its history to include operations that entail the possibility of assassination of chiefs of state? Why has the CIA proceeded to attempt two coups in Panama, followed by the gory pageantry of the December 1989 invasion?

The answer is that, despite the lofty rationales of the Cold War, the CIA never was Horatio standing at the bridge holding back the Communist hordes. Now more clearly than ever, the CIA, with its related institutions, is exposed as an agency of destabilization and repression. Throughout its history, it has organized secret wars that killed millions of people in the Third World who had no capability of doing physical harm to the United States.

Today, the United States is still very much a member of the global financial order, although bleeding heavily, and the Soviet Union is eager to join that order. A CBS "60-Minutes" show during the 1988 presidential election revealed that a dozen members of George Bush's campaign staff had recently accepted six-figure commissions from foreign corporations and governments. As an international businessman, Bush is deeply committed to world commerce, to the point of sacrificing the primary interests of the American people.

We have now come to the world of George Kennan's Haves versus Have Nots, with the United States cast in the role of Praetorian Guard, protecting the interests of the global financial order against fractious elements in the Third World. Under the thin guise of anti-Communism, the battles of the Cold War were actually fought in the Third World, where future conflicts will also be fought. Under President Carter, U.S. Rapid Deployment Forces held joint training exercises in Egypt; throughout the 1980s, the National Guard rotated units constantly on training exercises in Honduras.

In 1989, Bush was sworn into office facing grave national economic problems, the reputation for wimpiness, and the threat of exposure (and possible impeachment) for his role in the Iran/*contra* scandal. The latter was exacerbated by his former CIA contact, Manuel Noriega in Panama, who openly claimed he had the ability to blackmail George Bush. The Bush administration began "targeting" public opinion on Noriega. His CIA spent $10 million on the spring 1989 Panamanian elections, succeeding in voting Guillermo Endara into the presidency only to find that Noriega would not cede power to him. The Bush administration then upped the volume and tone of its public attack on Noriega. Watching this, it was not difficult, even in the early months of 1989, to predict that Bush would order the invasion of Panama if he could not succeed in ousting Noriega from power through a *coup d'état*. In December 1989, while the military wrecked havoc on Panama City, Bush demonstrated his *sang froid* by shooting quail at a friend's ranch in south Texas.

Still, with the national debt rapidly mounting, the standard of living falling, the military facing substantial cuts in its lion's share of the budget, and Bush unable to escape the Savings and Loan scandal, it was utterly predictable in the spring of 1990, well after Panama, that President Bush would need yet another major military adventure to sustain his leadership. The invasion cost the U.S. $2 billion, doing perhaps another $2 billion in damages to Panama, while killing more than 2,000 people. It was over in a week and it was clouded afterwards with inadequate justification—Noriega probably never can be brought to trial. Faced with grave, continuing economic problems, and encouraged by a desperate military establishment, President Bush would need a war that would be closer to Vietnam in size, destructiveness, and controversy.

Where then would the next war be staged? Nicaragua had been targeted for an invasion in the mid-1980s but could be ruled out after the recent U.S. "success" in the elections there and the Bush administration's numerous signals that it was no longer interested in the country. The United States could not return to Southeast Asia for military action, and Africa and Latin America simply would not sell to the American people.

Cuba remained, just 90 miles from U.S. shores, the last defiant Communist bastion, and a long-time designated enemy. President Bush averred that there would be no compromise, no improvement in relations as long as Fidel Castro was in power, and of course Castro, who has his own case of testosterone poisoning, would hardly step down because a seventh U.S. president didn't like him. Cuba would be a viable target for the required war. It is well enough defended that it would not be a pushover. However, it is close to the United States, and as an island can be blockaded and completely shut off. There would be no 900-mile-long Ho Chi Minh trail for resupply, and the Soviet Union, with it reversal of policies, would not try to support Cuba the way it had North Vietnam. To the contrary, the Soviet Union is rather desperately courting U.S. favor and seeking aid, while struggling to stave off internal economic and political collapse.

The familiar, noisy orchestration of opinion against Castro began in the Fall of 1989: public statements and an unbending policy by the President; continuous speeches and statements by the Vice-President; the construction of the TV-Marti station that is broadcasting into Cuba, provoking Castro; a constant drumbeat of articles in the media criticizing Castro. There were articles in Florida and east coast papers reporting that Cuban exiles were selling their businesses and banks, preparing to hit the ground in a post-Castro Cuba with liquid capital. Their bumper-stickers in the spring of 1990 read "Home Before Xmas!" Meetings were held by Cuban exile leaders and retired CIA operatives like Theodore Shackley, who commanded the JMWAVE station during the OPMONGOOSE secret war against Cuba, to discuss how the new post-Castro government would be organized. Meanwhile, the U.S. fleet was running training exercises off the coast of Cuba, rehearsing an invasion, its aircraft testing Cuba's defenses by feigning attacks. Clearly Cuba was being prepared for the next U.S. war.

Then came Iraq's invasion of Kuwait in August 1990, and President Bush had a better war, truly a "Good War" as Studs Terkel described World War II in his book of the same title. The invasion was a fact and Saddam Hussein's bloody history made him demonstrably "evil." The rationales were sufficiently convincing that long-time leaders in the peace movement supported or at least were not vigorously opposed to U.S. military intervention. Even Daniel Ellsberg, one of the historic leaders whose courageous acts helped to halt the Vietnam War, admits that initially he thought that a U.S. military reaction to Hussein might be appropriate. Hawkish others, including former Secretary of the Navy and Texas governor John Connally, even suggested that the United States should use nuclear weapons on Baghdad.

Neither Iraq's invasion of Kuwait nor Hussein's "evil" ways would have been adequate justification for expensive military action, *unless the United States had its own imperatives.* George Bush called the invasion "naked aggression," but Hussein had better historical rationales and objectives in Kuwait—and greater provocation—than Bush did in his own invasion of Panama seven months earlier. And the United States deals with brutal killers all across the globe, not the least of which is the leadership of Syria, a country that has invaded an inoffensive neighbor, Lebanon, and harbored terrorists who targeted Americans. Syria is now our ally against Iraq.

At stake in Kuwait and Saudi Arabia is 40 percent of the world's oil, and Iraq is in the process of developing a nuclear capability. With a competent army of 400,000 and thousands of tanks and jet fighter aircraft, the "match" was perceptibly fairer that Grenada and Panama, and the war promised to be large enough to be a major distraction. At the same time, U.S. military commanders felt it would be winnable in 90 days, or less, before domestic protest could gather momentum.

There is even evidence that, on the eve of his invasion of Kuwait, the U.S. ambassador to Iraq reassured Saddam Hussein that Kuwait would be outside the circle of grave U.S. concern. This raises the question of whether Hussein might even have been lured by the United States into the invasion. Remember, the CIA had been actively destabilizing Iraq through Kuwait, costing the country territory, oil fields, and billions of dollars in revenues. At the very least, Hussein was not discouraged or warned as he would have been had the U.S. not wanted him to invade; and for years he had enjoyed relations with and purchased arms from the U.S. He was a provisional ally.

At first, Bush's argument was that the war would be fought for cheap gasoline. Then it was to stop Hussein from developing atomic weapons. So flagrant has President Bush's orchestration to war been that he has even tied the Persian Gulf crisis to jobs in the United States and blamed Iraq for the U.S. recession. The latter argument is so preposterous that even the stridently hawkish columnist William Safire protested in a November 22, 1990 syndicated column.

U.S. economic problems are the result of long-term policies, over-spending on the military, and prolonged trade deficits. However people began to feel the pinch of recession after the invasion of Kuwait in August. President Bush seemed to believe that the public would be receptive to a "spin" that linked the two and faulted Hussein for problems at home.

In October and November 1990, the Center for Defense Information published its assessment that a Persian Gulf War was inevitable: that it would probably begin in early December or January 1990; that the U.S. strategy would be to feint attack against Iraqi defenses in Kuwait while concentrating its real attack on Iraq itself; that Iraqi air power would be eliminated in the first 72 hours; that the entire war would last about 90 days; that casualties would total 40,000 to 50,000; that the cost would be about $70 billion. Was it possible that the United States would use nuclear weapons? Admiral Carroll emphatically rejected that possibility, but noted that, if Hussein endeavored to divide the United States/Arab coalition that supports the invasion by firing his missiles at Tel Aviv, the Israelis might very well retaliate with nuclear strikes. When asked about the Kuwaiti oil fields that will likely suffer massive damage in the war, Carroll said that by attacking Iraq directly, the Bush administration apparently hoped that Hussein would be blamed for any damage to or sabotage of the oil fields.

With or without war between the United States and Iraq, the Bush administration, the military establishment, and the new world order that President Bush is proudly bringing together have accomplished a great deal in their own interests. The U.S. budgetary crisis has been taken off the front pages of the newspapers. President Bush has been able to forge a broad international coalition of support including Arab states, European industrial countries, and even the Soviet Union. And a military presence has been established in the Middle East.

The military has already seen its budget restored, to an all-time high, and it has strong, though fallacious, new rationales for continued dominance of U.S. society. The Third World is the new *enemy*, effectively replacing the Cold War rationales for militarism. The military must be restructured to fight wars in the Third World. Expensive new equipment to transport heavy armor rapidly across the globe is needed. Already massive orders have been placed for the resupply of munitions that will be used in the conflict (ignoring the massive reserves that were stockpiled in the $2.5 trillion buildup in the 1980s).

So, why should the U.S. *not* proceed with the Persian Gulf War to eliminate the evil Saddam Hussein, curtail his potential nuclear power, and punish the Iraqis for their militarism?

First, it should be noted that cheap gasoline has not and will not be a benefit of the Persian Gulf "crisis" and war. After Iraq's August invasion of Kuwait, profiteering immediately jerked gasoline prices upwards, even when there was no prospect of a shortage. Six months later, they had not gone back down. During a war, the Kuwaiti oil fields might well be destroyed and the 30,000 foreign technicians might well be obliged to withdraw, at least temporarily, from Saudi Arabia. The result could be real oil shortages and greatly increased prices. With U.S. and Soviet economies in deep trouble, the world economy itself is precarious. Exposing it to a major blow, involving serious disruption of the petroleum supplies, is at best risky.

Second, U.S. troops would do a lion's share of the fighting and dying, and the United States would bear the major part of the estimated $70 billion costs. Yet the oil at stake in Kuwait and Saudi Arabia is not U.S. oil. It belongs to the Kuwaiti and Saudi leaders. Most of it is sold to Germany and Japan. Nor would the owners of the oil or the purchasers supply significant numbers of troops or even substantially fund the war. The Japanese and Germans are more pragmatic—even should Saddam Hussein capture the Saudi oil, he cannot sell it except to them.

Third, the Saudi and Kuwaiti regimes whose interests the United States would defend at such a high cost cannot be described as worthy. They are not democracies, even by the most cynical U.S. standards. The film *Death of a Princess* reconstructed the harsh execution of the Saudi leader's nineteen-year-old granddaughter and her lover by firing squad in a public square, the punishment for pre-marital sex. Women are firmly repressed in Saudi Arabia. They cannot drive automobiles. Women soldiers in the U.S. Army in camps in the Saudi desert have been admonished to come and go through the back gates only. By no means does Saudi Arabia practice anything resembling religious tolerance. Families of U.S. soldiers are warned against sending Christian literature to their sons, daughters, and husbands, because it is prohibited and censored by Saudi law.

Finally, the long-term repercussions in the Arab world will not likely be favorable to the United States. Too many of the Moslem Arabs will deeply resent the entry of U.S. forces, fighting and killing other Arabs. The U.S. presence, and the governments of its key allies, all promise to be less stable as a result of such a war.

The United States cannot afford a $70 billion war that will

exacerbate budget and deficit problems. Renewed military dominance of U.S. society simply guarantees that the conditions that have cost the United States its status as an economic superpower and put it in such a deep hole will continue.

At the same time, it must never be forgotten that the Reagan/Bush adminstration of the 1980s created FEMA with its provisions to suspend the Constitution, impose martial law, and intern aliens and dissenters. The 45 percent of the federal judges who were appointed by President Reagan can be expected to enforce the new laws. Under the aegis of war, if there is substantial protest, even protest of economic and social problems, leaders will obviously be tempted to use those repressive laws against dissent at home. To presume they would not is to beg the question of why they created the infrastructure and the laws of repression in the first place.

President Bush is thus moving into the final consolidation phase of the cynical Reagan Revolution. In ushering in the new world order, President Bush may or may not be securing for himself a place in history, but he is surely serving global financial and security interests, not those of the United States itself. As the Praetorian Guard, fighting wars for multinational interests while also paying for such adventures, our relative economic stability, domestic social and material infrastructure, and the freedom and liberties of the American people may all be forfeited.

ARMAGEDDON

Since the 1950s, we have been told that thermonuclear weapons are safe, "fail-safe" they called them, and no cause for worry. Over the years, there have been many thousands of accidents and errors ranging from a nuclear explosion to a nuclear plant melt-down to hundreds of near-catastrophic misses. In one 12-month period in 1985-1986, the Challenger II blew up, a Delta rocket blew up, two Titan missiles blew up, a French Ariane missile blew up, the Chernobyl plant melted down, and a Soviet SS-18 blew up—and that was not a particularly bad year. We have dropped seven bombs accidentally out of airplanes. One over South Carolina was never found; they went in and bought a huge tract of swampland and declared it a "Nuclear Restricted Zone." Presumably, the bomb is still there in the brackish water, rusting—unless, of course, someone else has found it.

Six submarines have sunk into the bottom of the ocean. We recovered two, one of ours and one of the Soviets. That leaves four submarines at the bottom of the ocean, twisted and rusting, with their nuclear plants and nuclear weapons on board. The Institute for Policy Studies reported in the spring of 1991 that there is debris from 50 nuclear reactors and nuclear weapons scattered on the bottom of the ocean. There are hundreds of millions of gallons of radioactive waste that we have no idea what to do with which will still be toxic 50,000 years from now, and huge stockpiles of chemical and biological weapons. Biological weapons are often called the "poor man's atomic weapons" because non-industrial nations can produce and deliver them. A vial of some of these agents can kill everyone in a city of 50,000.

Integral in all of this is the systematic destruction of our environment. For example, during the Vietnam War, tons of Agent Orange were dropped, destroying primeval rain forests and poisoning the land. It is true that forests are growing back, but with a drastic reduction in the number and variety of trees. Lost, perhaps forever, are the ancient mahoganies that provided ecological continuity over centuries. Studies show that the variety of fauna is also substantially reduced. In parts of the Delta, fish yields are a fourth of what they were before the Vietnam War. EPOCA, and other groups that have done environmental studies of Central America, show a cynical misuse of the environment and destruction of the rain forests. For one thing, the local oligarchies that are so cynical about human life invariably seem to show comparable indifference to the environment, in preference to business interests and profits. Environmental degradation is systematic violence committed against the earth. As noted above, the Somoza family in Nicaragua, for example, among the prototypes of the U.S. policy of control-by-proxy, allowed corporations to do whatever they wanted as long as palms were greased. The result was that Nicaragua's two huge, beautiful lakes were poisoned for human use. In contrast, the first ministry created by the Sandinistas when they took power in Nicaragua in 1979 was that of the environment.

The mentality of exploitation that was demonstrated by the national security-minded President Reagan ("If you've seen one redwood, you've seen them all.") and his first Secretary of the Interior, James Watt, who opened millions of acres of federal land for exploitation. This callousness carried into the nuclear weapons industry. In recent years, the cynicism of nuclear plant managers has made a dent in the public consciousness. For 40 years, they used secrecy as the cover for criminal negligence in permitting and then covering up the leaking and dumping of toxic wastes. A classic case is the Pantex plant near Amarillo, Texas, where the managers could not find a convenient disposal for "hot" liquid wastes. They scooped flat tanks in the ground with bulldozers and dumped the toxic liquids in them to evaporate into the air, leak into the soil, and blow into surrounding fields. The Justice Department has announced that it is preparing to file criminal charges against some of the managers.

In her book, *Blessed Assurance: At Home with the Bomb in Amarillo,* A. G. Mojtabai demonstrates a keen eye for somber ambiguities. She notes that, in the city that supports the Pantex final assembly plant for U.S. thermonuclear weapons, there are a disproportionate number of churches; she observes that some of the ministers who preach that through the "bomb" God will be coming to take his chosen away also carry life insurance. Amarillo has more fireworks ordinances that any other city in the United States. And the environmentalists who count 52 endangered species in the Texas Panhandle do not include homo sapiens on their list.

CHALLENGE AND HOPE

Carl Sagan says a species divided against itself cannot survive, a planet divided against itself cannot survive. Eisenhower, in a speech as he was leaving office, said, "The people of the world genuinely want peace. Some day the leaders of the world are going to have to give in and give it to them."

Helen Caldicott challenges us, "Get involved. Your *planet* is at stake. It is terminally ill with this public health problem called the nuclear arms race. If we don't clean it up, the planet will die." And she notes, "If you will get to work on it you will feel better about yourself, your planet, your environment, and your life." Her final comment is that if you do get involved in working on the problems of the world, if the missiles start going off someday and there are a few minutes before one lands on your town, at least you can turn to your loved one and hug him or her and say, "Honey, at least we tried."

People have done dramatic things throughout history in the interest of positive social change. *Glasnost* is a tentative, in some ways misguided, step in the direction of stopping the madness of the arms race, stopping the race to Armageddon. It should give us hope if it is not perverted into a draconian, nuclear world order. Two other examples of social change are the Women's Movement in this country, and the case of the professor who stopped a war.

Eighty years ago, a man could put his wife, sisters, and daughters to work twelve hours a day, seven days a week in factories and then pocket their salaries. If they didn't like it, he could beat them, and there was little they could do about it. That situation has been changed dramatically—not by accident, but by the determined struggles of feminist activists. They accomplished their reforms without cracking skulls; they did it without killing people; they did it without violence. If the problem is essentially testosterone poisoning, as Carl Sagan and his wife Ann Druyea have called it in *Parade* Magazine articles, we are not going to solve the problem with more testosterone poisoning or more violence. We have to find a new way for human beings to deal with one another without violence, or we may self-destruct as a species.

The professor who stopped the war, my war in Angola, is a wonderfully inspiring example. Then young Professor Jerry Bender of the University of California, San Diego, who had done his studies in Angola, saw what we were doing. He agonized over what to do. How could he stop it? One day he picked up the telephone and he called his senator, and he said, "Senator Tunney, I have some expertise on Angola. I see what the CIA is doing, and I think they are lying to you. I think it is dangerous, and I would like the opportunity to brief you. I will not waste your time." The Senator listened to him and found that we were indeed lying to the Congress. He introduced the Tunney Amendment to the FY 76 Defense Appropriation Act, which stopped my war in Angola.

Some years ago, I went to talk to Admiral LaRocque at the Center for Defense Information in Washington to ask him what to say when people ask what they can do about the problem of the arms race. We were having breakfast at the Admiral's home, and this beautiful man who has served his country for over 50 years stood and said, "I love that question. I tell people, I don't know you, but you know yourselves. You know what your capabilities are. If you can write, write articles, write letters, write books, write telegrams. If you can organize, organize. If you can travel, go to Nicaragua or to the Las Vegas test sites and see for yourself so you can be an intelligent witness to what is happening in the world." He said, and I quote, "I tell people, if they feel comfortable lying down in front of trucks with bombs on them, to lie down in front of trucks with bombs on them. But," he said, "I tell them, 'You have got to do what you can do every day of your life. You cannot wait until you graduate next summer or get married or get divorced or get a job, because these nuclear weapons malfunction all the time, and they are controlled by fallible human beings like Ronald Reagan. The world may not *be* here by the time you graduate next summer or get divorced or get a job or whatever.'"

Truly it is time for the people of the world to join hands and find a solution to world conflict, to pressure the leaders into responding. "National security" must be replaced with concern for the fate of the earth. The human race must take a quantum, evolutionary leap forward, if it is to survive its own combative nature and avoid self-destruction.

FOOTNOTES

1. First established in 367 B.C., the Roman praetors evolved into the Praetorian Guard that came to exercise great power, making and unmaking emperors, allowing political and military action outside of the law and refusing to allow action that would lie within the *jus civile.* What rules were observed were announced by exercise of the *jus edicendi,* or the issuance of edicts. The Guard was characterized by corruption and political venality and was closed down by Constantine in 312 B.C.

2. Quoted in Howard Zinn, *A People's History of the United States,* New York: Harper and Row, 1989, p. 290.

3. *Newsweek,* May 23, 1988.

4. *Killing Our Own,* by Harvey Wasserman and Norman Solomon with Robert Alvarez and Eleanor Walters (New York: Delacorte, 1982) also records the hundreds of thousands of people who have been killed in official U.S. military and civilian experiments and blunders.

5. Of course, I am an ex-Marine recon officer. General P.X. Kelley, who as commandant was responsible for the deaths of 261 Marines in Beirut in 1983, was my commanding officer in the 2nd Force Recon Company in 1960-62.

6. For more about this contemptible chapter in U.S. history, see Frank Snepp's *Decent Interval,* New York: Random House, 1977.

7. The so called "secret wars" of the CIA are rarely if ever really secret. Sometimes our leaders maintain plausible or implausible deniability, but the victims certainly know they are being targeted, as do all seriously interested researchers

8. My own *In Search of Enemies* (New York: Norton, 1978) details the CIA's Angola program of 1975-1976. Gerald Bender's *Angola Under the Portuguese* (Berkeley: University of California Press, 1978), and John Marcum's *The Angolan Revolution, Volumes I and II* (Cambridge: M.I.T. Press, 1978) are comprehensive histories.

9. Perhaps the most abject demonstration of fealty to U.S. power was when El Salvadoran President José Napoleon Duarte,

who was also a long-time CIA collaborator, visited the White House in 1988 where he knelt and kissed the hem of the U.S. flag.

10. On the *contras*: *Contra Terror in Nicaragua* by Reed Brody (Boston: South End Press, 1985), the former Assistant Attorney General of New York State; *With the Contras* by Christopher Dickey (New York: Simon and Schuster, 1987), a so-called moderate journalist representing the *Washington Post* in Central America; *Washington's War on Nicaragua* by Holly Sklar (Boston: South End Press, 1988).

11. For more information about democracy in Nicaragua, see Michael Parenti's article in *Covert Action Information Bulletin* #25, Summer 1986.

12. For a clear explanation of this process, see Jonathan Kwitny's *Endless Enemies* (New York: Congdon and Weed, 1984). As a reporter for the *Wall Street Journal*, Kwitny witnessed a meeting of the Zairian foreign minister with New York bankers to refinance the country's massive loans. Despite flagrant mismanagement and economic insecurity, the loans were renegotiated. The bankers were willing to take the risk because the loans were guaranteed by U.S. taxpayers. The loaned money, in any event, never left New York City. It was transferred from one bank in Manhattan to a Zairian account in another bank in Manhattan. See also, Kwitny's second book, *The Crimes of Patriots* (New York: Norton, 1987), which exposed the CIA's corrupt financial proprietary, the Nugan Hand Bank. After its publication, Kwitny was pressured into resigning from the *Wall Street Journal*.

13. On the economics of the Indonesian operation, see Jonathan Kwitny's *Endless Enemies* (New York: Congdon and Weed, 1984).

14. Interested parties can read about it in greater detail by going to the voluminous reports of Amnesty International and to the U.S. congressional record. A. J. Langguth's *Hidden Terrors* (Pantheon, 1978) provides an excellent summary. For those who like to obtain their information visually, there are a number of films including Alan Francovich's *On Company Business* and *The Houses Are Filled with Smoke, State of Seige,* and Oliver

Stone's *Salvador.*

15. Still one of the best books about Korea is I.F. Stone's *The Hidden History of the Korean War* (New York: Monthly Review Press, 1952).

16. For more on the CIA's role in Vietnam, see William Blum's *The CIA: A Forgotten History* (London: Zed Publishers, 1986); *Portrait of a Cold Warrior* by Joseph Burkholder Smith (New York: Putnam, 1976), who was a CIA case officer in Southeast Asia; *Fire in the Lake* by Frances Fitzgerald (New York: Vintage, 1973), the daughter of Desmond Fitzgerald, the famous CIA Chief of Operations of Southeast Asia; *Decent Interval* by Frank Snepp (New York: Random House, 1977).

17. Noam Chomsky estimates the total number of people killed in U.S.-sponsored activities in Southeast Asia at four million.

18. For more information on MKULTRA, see *The Agency* by John Ranelagh (New York: Simon and Schuster, 1987); *Acid Dreams*, by Martin A. Lee and Bruce Shlain (New York: Grove, 1985); *Clouds of Secrecy* by Leonard A. Cole (Totowa, NJ: Rowman and Littlefield, 1988); *The Search for the "Manchurian Candidate"* by John Marks (New York: Times Books, 1979); or go through the back issues of *Covert Action Information Bulletin*, which has published a dozen solid articles about this program.

19. This brazen assertion, one of many by Colonel White, was included in an ABC television show by John Marks in 1979. White has since died.

20. As a counterintelligence specialist, and chief of base in Saigon, Johnson had helped to supervise offices that interrogated prisoners, where there were many reports of torture and duress. One of the latter was the case of a suspected North Vietnamese agent who was kept for seven years in a brightly lit, frigidly air-conditioned cell and never broke. According to Frank Snepp's *Decent Interval* (New York: Random House, 1977), the man was taken up in a helicopter and thrown out from a high altitude over the South China Sea at the suggestion of a CIA official in order to avoid adverse publicity in late April 1975, days before U.S. officials, including Mr. Johnson, fled.

21. For more information on the history of domestic covert operations—especially COINTELPRO—and strategies for handling political repression, see *Agents of Repression* by Ward Churchill and Jim Vander Wall (Boston: South End Press, 1990), *The COINTELPRO Papers* edited by Ward Churchill and Jim Vander Wall (Boston: South End Press, 1990), and *War at Home* by Brian Glick (Boston: South End Press, 1989).

22. The best single book on the drug war, of the dozen that are now coming out on the subject, is probably *The Crisis in Drug Prohibition,* edited by David Boaz (available for $8 from the CATO Institute, 224 Second St., SE, Washington, DC 20003). See also *Beyond the War on Drugs* by Steven Wisotsky (Buffalo, NY: Prometheus Books, 1990); "Drug Prohibition in the United States" by Ethan A. Nadelmann," *Science,* Vol. 245, September 1, 1989; "Is the Bill of Rights a Casualty of the War on Drugs?" a paper delivered by Eric Sterling to the 92nd meeting of the Colorado State Bar Association, September 14, 1990.

23. For more on the CIA drug connection, see Frontline's video, *Guns, Drugs, and the CIA,* or read *The Great Heroin Coup* by Henry Krüger (Boston: South End Press, 1980); *Nazi Gold* by Ian Sayer and Douglas Botting (London: Granada, 1984); *The Iran-Contra Connection* by Jane Hunter, Jonathan Marshall, and Peter Dale Scott (Boston: South End Press, 1987); *The Politics of Heroin in Southeast Asia* by Alfred W. McCoy (New York: Harper and Row, 1972); *The Cocaine Wars* by Paul Eddy, Hugo Sabogal, and Sara Walden Paul (New York: Norton, 1988); *The Senator Must Die* by Robert D. Morrow (Santa Monica, CA: Roundtable, 1988).

24. For more on the Kennedy assassination, see *Crossfire* by Jim Marrs (New York: Graf Carroll, 1989), which is probably the most comprehensive book on the assassination; *The Senator Must Die* by Robert D. Morrow (Santa Monica, CA: Roundtable, 1988); *Betrayal* by Robert D. Morrow (Chicago: H. Regnery, 1976); *On the Trail of Assassins* by Jim Garrison (New York: Sheridan Square Press, 1988); *Contract on America* by David E. Scheim (Silver Spring, MD: Argyle Press, 1983); *Reasonable Doubt* by Henry Hurt (New York: Holt, Rinehart, and Winston, 1986); *Best Evidence* by David S. Lifton (New York: Macmillan,

1980). Also see *Secrecy and Power* by Richard Gid Powers (New York: Free Press, 1987), in which you will learn that Richard Nixon had Mafia ties dating back to his first election campaign in California. The Mafia maintains connections in national politics to this day; it is a major, though quiet member of the establishment.

25. See *Trading With the Enemy* by Charles Higham (New York: Delacorte Press, 1983).

ANNOTATED BIBLIOGRAPHY

The foundation of democary must be knowledge, which is, by definition, the intellectual high ground! The truth speaks for itself. It is the cynics and the manipulators who lie and seek to burn books while we urge people to read and analyze.

In the past ten years alone, there has been a fabulous increase in knowledge about how the world really works, knowledge that was not available to my generation in our youth. I offer the following bibliography as evidence that there remains ground on which to build our hope for a better world.

The first book everyone should read in order to understand the United States, the American Way, and the new "World Order" the U.S. has formulated at the end of the Cold War is Howard Zinn's *A People's History of the United States,* New York: Harper and Row, 1989.

Exploitation for profit did not begin with the formation of the CIA after World War II. It began when Columbus landed in the Bahamas in 1492. Our histories traditionally recount events as they affected the dominant interests of our nation. Zinn re-examines those events from the bottom up illustrating how the system of American capitalism works, and in whose interests.

I: THE SELECTED LIST

The Crisis in Drug Prohibition edited by David Boaz. Available for $8 from the CATO Institute, 224 Second St., SE, Washington, DC 20003.

This collection of 27 essays ranks among the most concise and insightful contributions to Drug War scholarship. With only 148 pages, it is an ideal summary of the Drug War/Scam. Contributors to this anthology include Nobel laureate Milton Friedman, economist Thomas Sowell, journalist Anthony Lewis, conservative editor William F. Buckley, Jr., Russell Baker, Richard Cohen, Mike Ryoko, Mayor Kurt Schmoke, and writers for the *Economist* and the *Independent*.

Crossfire by Jim Marrs, New York: Graf Carroll, 1989.

In meticulous detail, this book destroys the "lone assassin" theory of President Kennedy's death, published by the Warren Commission in 1964. By 1963, the liberal Kennedy had antagonized the CIA (in the Bay of Pigs), the military industrial complex (by deciding to pull back from the planned war in Vietnam), the Mafia (by his and Robert Kennedy's vigorous investigation of organized crime), the FBI (because of its director's "understanding" with organized crime), conservative Dallas businessmen (by curtailing the oil depletion allowance), and the Deep South (with tentative civil rights reforms). By November 1963, there were numerous known plots to kill him. One of them involved the CIA, the Mafia, and military intelligence. The machinery that normally functions to protect the President was set aside to permit his ambush and killing in Dallas on November 22, 1963. It was nothing less than a *coup d'état*.

Declarations of Independence by Howard Zinn, New York: Harper Colophon, 1990.

Sigmund Freud and Harvard University's E.O. Wilson each wrote that history (not psychology or biology) proves the human compulsion to aggression. Thus Zinn concludes that we are socially, not genetically, programmed to violence.

The Fate of the Earth by Jonathan Schell, New York: Knopf, 1982.

Sit down and read this book today.

Schell discusses the First and the Second Deaths. The former is our death—yours, mine, the president's, the generals', the senators', and the bombmakers', in the holocaust, if it happens. The second death is of unborn generations of human-kind who will never have the opportunity to live because of our greed and foolishness.

In Search of Enemies: A CIA Story by John Stockwell, New York: Norton, 1978.

My first book, this remains the only detailed insider account of a major CIA covert action. The CIA sued me under the *Snepp* ruling of the Supreme Court, seized the proceeds from my book's sales, and put me under a court order requiring that future works must be submitted to the CIA for censorship.

Inevitable Revolutions: The U.S. in Central America by Walter Lafeber, New York: Norton, 1983.

The United States has had a fixation on Latin and Central America—brutal, greedy, and racist—for 150 years. Today, the decades of U.S. intervention, destabilization, militarization, and subsidized drug smuggling have produced a Central America more dangerous, more bloody, and more revolutionary than anytime in its history.

Killing Our Own: The Disaster of America's Experience with Atomic Radiation by Harvey Wasserman and Norman Solomon with Robert Alvarez and Eleanor Walters, New York: Delacorte, 1982.

Wasserman and Solomon offer a comprehensive body count of the people who have been killed, and are still dying, as victims of the production and testing of nuclear weapons and the construction of nuclear power plants.

Manufacturing Consent: The Political Economy of the Mass Media by Noam Chomsky and Edward S. Herman, New York: Pantheon, 1988.

This book explains how the U.S. establishment sets the agenda for public debate and offers a narrow choice of acceptable answers in order to obtain a consensus that works to concentrate power and resources in the hands of the few.

New Perspectives Quarterly, Vol. 4, No. 3, published by the Institute for National Strategy, 11500 W. Olympic Blvd., Suite 302, Los Angeles, CA 90064.

To pursue the arms race, the United States is allocating

giant portions of available capital, scientific talent, and trade skills to the production of arms, thereby rendering itself non-competitive with Asian and European countries in the production of trade goods. This is highly profitable to the defense corporations but reduces the number of jobs available to people in the United States and is disastrous to the nation's long-term security. As a result, trade deficits have skyrocketed, the United States has become a debtor nation, and social services have been slashed.

Nuclear Power for Beginners by Stephen Croall and Kaianders Sempler, London: Writers and Readers, 1980.

Racing On? The New Handbook for the Changing Arms Race by John Stockwell and Dan Thibodeau, WECAN (ms), 1989.

For those who simply do not have time to read lots of books on the arms race, this is our effort to render the history, the major issues, and the big lies of the nuclear arms race in the most succinct form with 100 graphic illustrations. It endeavors to relay answers from qualified scientists to busy people. For example, What's wrong with Star Wars? and What difference have *glasnost* and the Intermediate Nuclear Forces Treaty made?

Shattered Peace: The Origins of the Cold War and the National Security State by Daniel Yergin, Boston: Houghton Mifflin, 1977.

In 1945-1947, when the Soviet threat was used to justify the creation of the CIA, the Soviet Union was on its knees from the destruction of World War II, but our system needed enemies in order to flourish. Today, with the end of the Cold War—presto!—the War on Drugs is used as an effective justification for everything from the showy invasion of Panama to new restrictions on civil liberties.

Trading With the Enemy: An Exposé of the Nazi-American Money Plot by Charles Higham, New York: Delacorte Press, 1983.

This book is based on U.S. government documents that were declassified under the Freedom of Information Act. It documents that as the winds of World War II began to blow, world financial leaders formed a bank in Switzerland that would be inviolate, whatever the outcome. Nazi leaders were permitted to invest $378 million they had looted from conquered Europe and gold they had stripped from the corpses of murdered Jews in the death camps. Standard Oil, owned by the Rockefeller family, sold oil to the Germans at better prices than to the United States. ITT, an American corporation with German subsidiaries, built the Focke-Wulfes that bombed British and U.S. forces. The vice chairman of the United States War Production Board colluded with Goering's cousin to ship ball bearings to German allies. Both Hitler and Roosevelt were powerless against this international financial elite.

Turning the Tide: U.S. Intervention in Central America and the Struggle for Peace by Noam Chomsky, Boston: South End Press, 1985.

Chomsky describes the United States' brutal Third World policies in terms of hegemony. Countries that try to escape domination must either be brought forcibly back under control or crushed so they will not stand as positive examples tempting others to break free.

II: THE DRUG WAR/SCAM

Beyond the War on Drugs: Overcoming a Failed Public Policy by Steven Wisotsky, Buffalo, NY: Prometheus Books, 1990.

A professor of law at Nova University Law Center gives us this comprehensive book on drugs. Criminalizing a minor health problem has harmed society far more than drugs themselves. Most of the drug-related crime, e.g., the organized crime bonanza estimated at $100 billion annually, the emergence of crack gangs, the corruption of law enforcement, etc., are the direct result not of drugs themselves, but of the War on Drugs. Criminalizing artificially inflates the price of cocaine 40-fold, creating an enormous "crime tariff" collected by the traffickers. In effect, the policy rewards smugglers for breaking the law, placing huge amounts of investment capital in their hands for the purpose of bribing and assassinating officials and purchasing legitimate businesses.

Dealing with Drugs: the Consequences of Government Control edited by Ronald Hamowy, San Francisco: Pacific Research Institute for Public Policy, 1987.

This book includes chapters by eleven of the brightest minds in the field. Of these Jonathan Marshall's "Drugs and United States Foreign Policy" provides an outstanding summation of how drug control provides rationales for brutal U.S. intervention in foreign countries, how the CIA has formed alliances with traffickers at home and abroad, e.g. Cuban exiles, Nicaraguan *contras,* Afghan opium smugglers.

"Drug Prohibition in the United States: Costs, Consequences, and Alternatives," by Ethan A Nadelmann, *Science,* Vol. 245, September 1, 1989.

This article covers much of the same ground as Professor Wisotsky's book. In 1985, 3562 people were known to have died in the United States from the use of all illegal drugs combined (not one from marijuana), or about the same number the EPA estimated died from passive cigarette smoking. The total number of people killed directly or indirectly each year from cigarettes and alcohol is estimated to be between 370,000 and 520,000. Although the Drug Warriors trumpet the costs of drug abuse, they downplay the costs of prohibition. Every police officer assigned to enforce the state's morality on the populace is unavailable to investigate murder, arson, robbery, rape, car theft, the S & L fraud, etc.

The Emperor Has No Clothes by Jack Herer and Chris Conrad, Queen of Clubs Publishing, 1990.

Did you know that hemp (marijuana) was a major trade item at the time of World War II? It is an excellent source of paper, rope, food protein, fuel, and oxygen-exchange (a potential help with the greenhouse effect). When our sources in the Pacific were threatened by the war, the government subsidized its domestic cultivation. Its growth has been officially encouraged for over 200 years. Benjamin Franklin started one of America's first paper mills with cannabis, and Hempstead Counties in Arkansas and Texas, Hemphill, North Carolina and

Hemphill, Texas were all named after cannabis.

"Is the Bill of Rights a Casualty of the War on Drugs?" a paper delivered by Eric Sterling to the 92nd Annual Convention of the Colorado Bar Association, Aspen, Colorado, September 14, 1990.

As a professor of law at American University, Sterling wrote much of the anti-crime and anti-drug legislation before acknowledging the futility and enormous costs of prohibition. In 1989 he founded the Criminal Justice Policy Foundation dedicated to ending the Drug War. In this paper he analyzes amendment by amendment how the Drug War undermines the Bill of Rights.

"Essentially the legal basis for the war on drugs depends upon the assumption of total power by the Congress and the Federal Government to regulate the most intimate aspects of our lives, the very dreams that we have...." he concludes.

A Law Unto Itself: Power, Politics, and the IRS by David Burnham, New York: Random House, 1989.

If information is power, then the Internal Revenue Service is the world's most powerful bureaucracy. Burnham worked for *Newsweek, CBS, UPI,* and the *New York Times* before writing this exposé. A tribute to independent journalism, this book examines the function of the Internal Revenue Service in maintaining the U.S. system of real existing capitalism. Its primary job is collecting legal revenues, but it also wields enormous power in its ability to seize property without due process and to give or take away exemptions according to an often vague and unfathomable set of laws. In turn, this has given it the power of selective enforcement, which it uses to reward friends and punish critics.

Burnham quotes Emil Poggi, who worked as a special agent in the IRS Criminal Investigation Division: "My colleagues and I worked zealously to enforce tax laws passed by Congress, although many of us were convinced that those laws were largely legalized deceptions that encouraged wealthy individuals and corporations to escape with little or no tax payment while the middle class and the poor pay punitive taxes to make up the deficiency."

Licit and Illicit Drugs by Edward M. Brecher and the editors of *Consumer Reports*, Boston: Little, Brown, and Company, Boston, 1972.

A comprehensive study of the pharmacology, sociology, and legal history of drugs, including narcotics, stimulants, depressants, inhalants, psychedelics, marijuana, caffeine, nicotine, and alcohol. This text is indispensable to understanding the current debate over "dangerous" drugs.

"The Tasks Ahead III: Problems of Population Control," by Noam Chomsky, *Zeta Magazine*, November 1989.

The "unsettling specter of peace" raises "knotty 'peace' questions," the *Wall Street Journal* observes. Chomsky examines the new, post-Cold War challenge to the nation's war machinery of sustaining the martial spirit among the population.

III: THE HUMAN RACE TO OBLIVION

Blessed Assurance: At Home with the Bomb in Amarillo, Texas by A. G. Mojtabai, Boston: Houghton Mifflin, 1986.

Mojtabai, an East Coast professor and writer, travelled to Amarillo, Texas, to examine the rationales of the people who live and work in the shadow of the final assembly plant of all U.S. nuclear weapons. Many, she found, subscribe to the Late Great Planet Earth scenario: God is coming soon to take his chosen away and will use the Bomb to create "Hell's Fires On Earth" for the unchosen. Mojtabai has a keen eye for ambiguities: advocates of the above who carry life insurance; the dozens of fireworks ordinances in the city that hosts the final assembly plant for all U.S. bombs; the environmentalists who count 52 endangered species in the Panhandle, but ironically do not include *homo sapiens* on their lists.

Day of the Bomb: Countdown to Hiroshima by Dan Kurzman, New York: McGraw-Hill, 1986.

This excellent book is unquestionably the best study of the personalities in the U.S., Germany, and Japan that were involved in the production of the atomic bomb.

The General and the Bomb by William Lauren, New York: Dodd Mead, 1988.

General Leslie Groves drove the Manhattan Project to its goal of producing usable atomic bombs before the end of World War II with ruthless efficiency. He took breathtaking gambles that were brilliantly vindicated. His responsibilities ranged from the Los Alamos Project to spy activities behind enemy lines in Europe, and to the Shingolobwe mines in the Congo (now Zaire). He delivered strategic uranium to the Soviet Union.

A fascinating account, in spite of the front cover flap, which asserts speciously that the building of the bomb saved "millions of lives."

The Making of the Atomic Bomb by Richard Rhodes, New York: Simon and Schuster, 1986.

This Pulitzer Prize-winning book is the most detailed account of the development of the atomic bomb, interweaving the personalities with the technology of the Manhattan Project.

Missile Envy: The Arms Race and Nuclear War by Helen Caldicott, New York: Morrow, 1984.

Caldicott, an important anti-nuclear leader, recounts a conversation with President Reagan in the Oval Office that revealed an awesome truth: the person with his finger on the proverbial Button simply did not understand much about missiles and such!

The Myth of Soviet Military Supremacy by Tom Gervasi, New York: Harper and Row, 1986.

Ronald Reagan successfully persuaded the U.S. public that the Soviet Union had outstripped the United States and established a military superiority, necessitating gigantic defense expenditures in order to catch up.

This claim was not true. The Soviets' forces were not superior. Gervasi bluntly refutes the big lies, explains their purposes, and gives the truth of the U.S. military advantage. He also notes that our advantage is irrelevant since no one can win a nuclear war.

The Nuclear Barons by Peter Pringle and James Spigelman, New

York: Holt, Rinehart and Winston, 1981.

At first, we were in a desperate struggle to get the Bomb before Hitler did. Then, when we *knew* that neither Hitler nor Imperial Japan nor the Soviet Union were developing the Bomb, we raced to finish ours before the war could end.

The Nuclear Cage: A Sociology of the Arms Race by Lester R. Kurtz, Englewood Cliffs, NJ: Prentice Hall, 1988.

We have locked ourselves in a cage of myths, beliefs, commitments, secrecy, discipline, and technology of the nuclear arms race from which an escape will not be simple. Understanding its bonds must be our first step toward freedom.

Nuclear War—What's In It For You? by Ground Zero, New York: Pocket Books, 1982.

"This story will not be reported on your evening news...." (There will no longer be any evening news, nor people to watch it.)

IV: THE ENVIRONMENT

AIDS: The HIV Myth by Jad Adams, New York: St. Martins, 1989.

For twenty years, the U.S. National Institutes of Health (NIH) spent hundreds of millions of dollars in a futile effort to prove that viruses were the universal cause of cancer. When they failed, its scientists postulated that perhaps it took the viruses two decades or longer to do their alleged thing. By the end of the 1970s, appropriately, the viral empire was greatly trimmed, leaving sufficient facilities to monitor the long-term studies.

Then came AIDS in the early 1980s. Present in many but not all cases was the HIV virus. The French developed a test for HIV; the NIH apparently pirated the French test—it was a profitable commodity in more ways than just its sale. Meanwhile an intense and successful program was launched to establish the unproven thesis that HIV *caused* AIDS. In time the NIH's viral empire was restored; the total budget to research and combat AIDS was $1.4 billion.

Jad Adams found that HIV was present in only 80 percent of the AIDS cases. In fact, more AIDS victims had Hepatitis-B than HIV. Many who tested positive to HIV did not die. Many who died of AIDS did not show HIV. In no case has the NIH been able to induce AIDS symptoms with HIV.

The NIH blamed the tests. They also vigorously discouraged research into other possible causes of AIDS. They postulated that maybe it took the virus decades to work. If in fact AIDS is caused by other conditions or micro-organisms, as is possible, then the NIH's policies will greatly delay the isolation of the real villain. Dr. Shih Lo, of the U.S. Army Institute of Pathology in Maryland, has isolated a virus-like micro-organism with which he *has* induced AIDS. His findings have been confirmed, but he has stubbornly resisted efforts by the NIH to take over the project. (Yes, the total cynics note that the U.S. Army Institute of Pathology is not far from the U.S. Army offices that hosted much of the MKULTRA experimentation.)

Design for a Liveable Planet: How You Can Help Clean Up the Environment by Jon Naar, New York: Harper and Row Publishers, 1990.

This book is about the decisions we make collectively and individually and the environmental crisis. Naar presents chapters on the garbage crisis, the toxic waste time bomb, the polluted waters and air, acid rain, deforestation, global warming, and radiation. He offers insightful analyses of the obstacles to saving the planet, including mindless patterns of investment and consumption, corporate greed, the Cartesian approach to nature, and entrenched special interest groups represented by prominent political leaders across the political spectrum such as Presidents Ronald Reagan and George Bush, Texas governor Ann Richards, and many others.

The $100 billion price tag of the Trident II nuclear submarine program, the world's most advanced first-strike weapon, amounts to one-third of the estimated clean-up cost for U.S. toxic waste dumps. The $79 billion squandered on the F-16 fighter and B-2 bomber equals 80 percent of the estimated costs to meet U.S. clean-water goals by the year 2000.

Naar points out that, "Workers at companies such as Grumman could turn their talents back to making wind turbines and solar thermal collectors, instead of unproductive weapons for a war that need never be fought."

Diet for a New America: How Your Food Choices Affect Your Health, Happiness, and the Future of Life on Earth by John Robbins, Walpole, New Hampshire: Stillpoint Publishing, 1987.

The author was to assume leadership of the Baskin-Robbins empire but declined after realizing the benefits of vegetarianism. He observes that our American consumption of meat results in the greatly increased incidence of various forms of cancer, osteoporosis, heart disease, hypertension, diabetes, hypoglycemia, multiple sclerosis, ulcers, intestinal problems, obesity, arthritis, kidney and gall stones, anemia, asthma, and salmonellosis. The production of meat pumps tons of poisons into the environment, causes erosion of the topsoil, depletes water aquifers, and leads to deforestation. It also wastes an enormous amount of energy, leading to military conflict over available supplies of oil.

For example, it takes an average of 2,500 gallons of water to produce one pound of meat. Without numerous state and federal subsidies to the meat industry, hamburger would cost $35 per pound. In 1960, when the United States first began to import beef from Central America, that region was blessed with 130,000 square miles of virgin rain forest. By 1985, less than 80,000 square miles remained.

Robbins concludes, "A nonviolent world has its roots in a nonviolent diet."

Exploited Earth: Britain's Aid and the Environment by Teresa Hayter, London: Earthscan Publications, 1989.

This book examines the impact of Britain's aid on the global environment, showing why and how it must be changed.

The Fragmented Forest: Island Biogeography Theory and the Preservation of Biotic Diversity by Larry D. Harris, Chicago: University of Chicago Press, 1984.

This timely work will deeply concern and also warm the hearts of people who love trees and appreciate the life-giving oxygen and beauty they bring to our planet.

The Population Explosion: From Global Warming to Rain Forest Destruction, Famine, and Air and Water Pollution, Why Overpopulation is Our #1 Environmental Problem by Paul R. and Anne H. Ehrlich, New York: Simon and Schuster, 1990.

In 1968, when the earth's human population was only 3.5 billion, these two professors published their historic book, *The Population Bomb.* Now there are 5.3 billion people, growing by 95 million per year, threatening the earth's life support systems. Overpopulation contributes substantially to the problems of famine, global warming, acid rain, war, poverty, pollution, the garbage crisis, and desertification.

Not only overpopulation, but the way significant numbers of the people live amplifies the problem. The authors note, "Overpopulation in rich nations obviously represents a much greater threat to the health of Earth's ecosystems than does population growth orientation in poor countries."

State of the World: a Worldwatch Institute Report on Progress Toward a Sustainable Society, New York: Norton, annual since 1984.

Excellent data on the current state of the environment and the rate of its destruction.

Our Common Future by the World Commission on Environment and Development, Oxford University Press, 1990.

Most of today's decisionmakers will be dead before the planet suffers the full consequences of acid rain, global warming, ozone depletion, widespread desertification, and species loss. Most of today's young voters, however, will be alive. The time has come for a marriage of economy and ecology, so that governments and their people can take responsibility not just for environmental damage, but for the policies that cause the damage.

V: THE ROOTS OF U.S. "NATIONAL SECURITY" COMPULSIONS

The American Police State: The Government Against the People by David Wise, New York: Random House, 1976.

A useful examination of the rationales and controls of the national security managers. Since this book was written, numerous laws have been passed, strengthening the power of security agencies at the expense of civil liberties.

At Home: Essays 1982-1988 by Gore Vidal, New York: Random House, 1988.

Typically brilliant and chilling in its presentation of the United States' inexorable drift into the national security state.

The Case for Hanging Errant Public Officials by James Farrell, San Francisco: Fulton Hall, 1988.

This book, by an arch-conservative, retired U.S. Air Force officer and advocate of the conservative Liberty Lobby, blasts the military-industrial complex for its cynicism. His views on other matters, however, tend toward sexism, xenophobia, and other insensitivities.

The Culture of Terrorism by Noam Chomsky, Boston: South End Press, 1988.

Franklin Delano Roosevelt asserted Four Freedoms which World War II was allegedly fought to protect: of speech, of worship, from want, and from fear. Chomsky asserts that U.S. policy since has been designed to defend a Fifth Freedom: to rob, exploit, and dominate, to undertake any course of action the United States chooses, however brutal, to ensure that its imperial privilege is protected and advanced.

The First Casualty: From the Crimea to Vietnam: The War Correspondent as Hero, Propagandist, and Mythmaker by Phillip Knightley, New York: Harcourt Brace Jovanovich, 1975.

Truth is the first casualty of any war. This fascinating history of war correspondents uncovers the role of the press and the suppression of information in the United States and Great Britain.

The Price of Power: Kissinger in the Nixon White House by Seymour Hersh, New York: Summit Books, 1983.

In the White House during the Nixon administration, Henry Kissinger would sit up past midnight, personally studying maps and selecting the Cambodian villages the U.S. Air

Force would "secretly" bomb the next day. This book is a comprehensive exposé of Henry Kissinger's manipulations, his "Track II" overthrow of the democratically elected government in Chile in 1973, his deceit in the SALT talks with Soviet negotiators, and his frequent consideration of the use of nuclear weapons in response to remote challenges in the Middle East or Asia.

Secrets of the Temple: How the Federal Reserve Runs the Country by William Greider, New York: Simon and Schuster, 1987.

Very few people realize that our monetary system is not controlled by elected politicians, but by the very secretive, semi-private Federal Reserve Board. Greider, a writer for *Rolling Stone*, offers details on how the board works.

To Serve the Devil, Volumes I and II, by Paul Jacobs and Saul Landau with Eve Pell, New York: Random House, 1971.

Historical accounts of the callous misuse of minorities, Indians, and the peoples of less powerful nations.

Shootdown: Flight 007 and the American Connection by R. W. Johnson, New York: Viking, 1986.

Bookstores in New York offered guarantees with this book: if the reader was not convinced that the ill-fated KAL 007 passenger flight that was shot down over sensitive Soviet missile facilities near Sakhalin on September 1, 1983 was on a spy mission, they would refund the purchase price.

Johnson puts the odds at about one in a trillion that all of the mistakes necessary to explain the airliner's errant course could have been accidental.

"The Target Is Destroyed": What Really Happened to Flight 007 and What America Knew About It by Seymour Hersh, New York: Random House, 1986.

Those who believe the KAL 007 flight was on an espionage overflight mission will receive no encouragement from this book. Hersh, who is one of the premier investigative journalists in the United States, concluded that there was no intelligence connection. Instead, what interested him was the ruthless cynicism with which the Reagan presidency seized upon the terrible incident to humiliate the Soviet Union in the eyes of the world, poisoning superpower communications and putting the world on the brink of World War III.

Trilateralism: The Trilateral Commission and Elite Planning for World Management edited by Holly Sklar, Boston: South End Press, 1980.

Europe, the United States, and Japan plot the economic fate of the industrial world.

The Washington Connection and Third World Fascism by Noam Chomsky and Edward S. Herman, Boston: South End Press, 1979.

The United States supports Third World dictators as they repress their peoples and steal billions of dollars from their countries' coffers. This book also offers a media critique and observes the difference between "benign" and "constructive" terror.

VI: COVERT OPERATIONS

The Agency: The Rise and Decline of the CIA by John Ranelagh, New York: Simon and Schuster, 1987.

More or less the official history of the CIA, determined to present its activities in a generally favorable light. It nevertheless includes some useful chronology of who held which high CIA office at which times, and invaluable corroboration of information about important CIA operations, like the MKULTRA drugs-and-disease experimentation on U.S. citizens.

The Armies of Ignorance: The Rise of the American Intelligence Empire by William R. Corson, New York: Dial Press, 1977.

This is probably the most comprehensive history and analysis of the CIA in print.

Blowback: America's Recruitment of Nazis and Its Effects on the Cold War by Christopher Simpson, New York: Weidenfeld and Nicolson, 1988.

A detailed account of how U.S. intelligence turned to Nazi

Gestapo and intelligence officers for help in running operations against the Russians in Europe even before World War II ended. They allowed one former Nazi, Reinhard Gehlen, to help define the U.S. policy that quickly evolved into the Cold War and the nuclear arms race by reporting fictional Soviet plans to invade Western Europe in what would have been World War III.

The CIA: A Forgotten History: U.S. Global Interventions Since World War II by William Blum, London: Zed Publishers, 1986.

This meticulously researched book documents and details 48 areas of major CIA covert actions. One of the best summaries of covert operations yet available.

The CIA and the Cult of Intelligence by Victor Marchetti and John D. Marks, New York: Dell, 1983.

An important book by a former administrator in the CIA Deputy Director's outer offices, privy to many of his secrets. Marchetti reports that at one time the CIA Director considered a public admission that some CIA field agents had been involved in the Kennedy assassination.

The CIA Sabotage Manual

Never overtly published, this indispensible reference for determined researchers is an illustrated "How-to" manual on sabotaging typewriters, trucks, sewers, etc., in order to destabilize a society, done in a comic book format. It was distributed in Nicaragua by CIA agents. Since it has never been formally published, obtaining copies is tricky. At one time the Washington Office on Latin America had some.

Covert Action: The Limits of Intervention in the Postwar World by Gregory F. Treverton, New York: Basic Books, 1987.

A restrained critique of the place of covert action in U.S. society.

Covert Action Information Bulletin, Issues 1-25, 1968-1986, Washington, DC: Covert Action Publications.

These provide more information about the complete scope of the national security complex, its myths, rationales, secret wars, media manipulations, and abuses, than anything else in print.

For example, they provide excellent articles on the CIA's

MKULTRA and other mind-control, drug, disease and chemical/biological weaponry experimentation programs.

The Craft of Intelligence by (a ghost writer for) Allen Welsh Dulles, New York: Harper and Row, 1963.

A "white" propaganda piece, published in the name of the one of the most famous CIA directors.

The Crimes of Patriots: A True Tale of Dope, Dirty Money, and the CIA by Jonathan Kwitny, New York: Norton, 1987.

This meticulously detailed book describes the Nugan-Hand bank that the CIA created and used to launder funds and drug money in the Pacific Basin until its founders became liabilities. One was murdered, while the other disappeared.

Decent Interval: An Insider's Account of Saigon's Indecent End by Frank Snepp, New York: Random House, 1977.

As South Vietnam fell in 1975, CIA case officers fled their posts in panic, leaving behind not only their Vietnamese employees, but also the files that identified those employees. The CIA station chief, Tom Polgar, discouraged realistic planning and preparations for an orderly evacuation of the South, and most of the CIA's Vietnamese employees were left behind. However, Polgar was also briefing the Hungarian Communist colonels assigned to Vietnam with the International Peacekeeping Commission, showing them secret CIA charts and files in the process. The Hungarian colonels were delivering this intelligence windfall to the North Vietnamese. Upon returning to Washington, Polgar was honored with the command of the CIA's largest field station, in Mexico City. In 1987, he was brought into the congressional team in Washington that was investigating the Iran/MIcontra scandal.

Dirty Work: The CIA in Western Europe edited by Philip Agee and Louis Wolf, Secaucus, NJ: Lyle Stuart, 1978.

Dirty Work 2: The CIA in Africa edited by Ellen Ray, Secaucus, NJ: Lyle Stuart, 1979.

Compendia of essays edited by three long-time CIA critics.

Fire Power by Chris Dempster and Dave Tomkins with Michel Parry, London: Corgi, 1978.

Mercenaries are often used when the CIA needs to deny U.S. involvement. This is the candid account of two British mercs hired by the CIA to fight in Angola in 1975.

Hearings Before the Select Committee to Study Government Operations With Respect to Intelligence Activities of the United States Senate, 94th Congress, First Session, 1975, volumes I-VII.

Known as the Church Committee reports, these are still the most important exposé of CIA covert operations. In the volume on covert action, the committee reports that the CIA was found to have run 900 major covert actions and several thousand minor operations in the preceding 14 years. Senator Frank Church (D) Iowa thought he would be able to close the CIA down, or at least halt its more brutal activities, but the CIA survived the exposure, retrenched, and eventually ousted Church from the Senate.

Inside the Company: CIA Diary by Philip Agee, New York: Bantam, 1975.

An all-time bestseller on the subject, this was the first major exposé, by a CIA insider, of CIA criminal activity in Latin America. Agee is the most controversial of the ex-CIA authors and has sacrificed the most, spending 15 years in exile in order to expose the CIA. In a one-man effort to stop its mayhem, he revealed specific agents and operations.

The Invisible Government by David Wise and Thomas B. Ross, New York: Random House, 1964.

The first big book warning that the United States government, supposedly "of, by, and for the people," was being eclipsed by the shadowy powers of the national security complex.

The Man Who Kept the Secrets: Richard Helms and the CIA by Thomas Powers, New York: Knopf, 1979.

This book is superbly written, its title a tongue-in-cheek reference to CIA Director Richard Helms, who was caught lying to the Senate about the CIA operation that killed Chilean President Allende. When Helms was indicted and threatened with conviction for that perjury, he made it quite clear that in order to save himself, he would make public every dirty secret he knew. The threat was enough. Helms was permitted to plea-bargain a suspended sentence plus a fine that the CIA exes' association paid for him.

Manhunt by Peter Maas, New York: Random House, 1986.

This is the remarkable story of the investigation and capture of Ed Wilson, one of the most notorious CIA and Naval Intelligence operatives. Wilson managed to build a $15 million estate from arms dealings with the help and encouragement of high CIA and Pentagon officials, including General Richard Secord (who was indicted in the Iran/*contra* scandal of 1986), Theodore Shackley, Eric Von Marbod, Thomas Clines, and numerous others.

Nazi Gold: The Story of the World's Greatest Robbery—and Its Aftermath by Ian Sayer and Douglas Botting, London: Granada, 1984.

During the collapse of Nazi Germany, the equivalent of $2.5 billion in gold and jewels disappeared from the Reichsbank, much of it into the hands of enterprising U.S. officials. This book describes the U.S. military occupation of conquered Germany as one of the most corrupt and exploitative occupations in history. Military law was arbitrary, nearly any enterprising soldier was able to obtain perquisites like commandeered houses and vehicles, and German women were considered fair game. In this dissolute environment, it is easier to understand how free-wheeling intelligence operatives could turn to Nazis for help in organizing intelligence operations (see *Blowback* above).

On the Run by Philip Agee, Secaucus, NJ: Lyle Stuart, 1987.

This book addresses the full adventure of this unique man's life: his mind, morality, and loneliness as he broke with his native land; fear and desperation as he was hounded from country after country by the CIA; courage and humor as he confronted some of his tormentors; love stories as he lost one lovely woman and then was rescued from statelessness by a brave, famous ballerina.

The Penkovskiy Papers by (??), New York: Avon Books, 1965.

Avon would have us believe that this book, highly flattering of American intelligence, is the authentic autobiography of Oleg Penkovskiy, the CIA's most famous spy, written while Penkovskiy was under maximum security on death row in a Soviet prison awaiting execution.

The Perfect Failure: Kennedy, Eisenhower, and the CIA at the Bay of Pigs by Trumbull Higgins, New York: Norton, 1987.

A concise account of the CIA's Bay of Pigs fiasco which "from the very beginning held the seeds of its own destruction." Brutally attacked and terrorized, destabilized by the CIA (working out of the JMWAVE offices on the University of Miami campus), the Cuban people rallied to support Fidel Castro.

The Pike Committee Report, New York: The Village Voice, undated.

While Senator Church investigated CIA covert action, in 1975 Congressman Pike examined the CIA's hidden budget and its performance in the production of intelligence, which Pike summarized in a word: "lousy." The CIA managed to generate enough support in Congress to suppress the publication of Pike's full report, but Pike leaked his major points to the *Village Voice.*

The Politics of Heroin in Southeast Asia by Alfred W. McCoy, New York: Harper and Row, 1972.

The French intelligence service, dominated by the Corsican Mafia, funded its operations in Southeast Asia by monopolizing the flow of heroin out of the Golden Triangle. When the French hold on Southeast Asia was broken in the battle of Dienbienphu (Vietnam) in 1954, the CIA quickly took over the operation, using the same airstrips and delivering to the same drug moguls, but using its own airlines, Civil Air Transport and Air America. The first market for the drugs was eventually among the U.S. GI's fighting in Vietnam. The second market of course was the United States.

Portrait of a Cold Warrior by Joseph Burkholder Smith, New York: Putnam, 1976.

The testimony of a CIA case officer who served in Vietnam. Provides insights into the destabilization that led the United States into the Vietnam War and some of the truth about the CIA's bloody destabilization of Indonesia in 1957-58.

Presidents' Secret Wars: CIA and Pentagon Covert Operations Since World War II by John Prados, New York: W. Morrow, 1986.

Another excellent summary of CIA destabilizations, organized by the presidential administrations that approved them.

Psychological Operations in Guerrilla Warfare, with essays by Joanne Omang and Aryeh Neier, New York: Vintage Books, 1985.

This is the famous "Assassination Manual" used by the CIA in training the *contras* in Honduras for their attacks on Nicaragua. President Reagan acknowledged this document in his television debates with Walter Mondale during the 1984 presidential election campaign. The manual has been republished in this book, with commentary by Joanne Omang and Aryeh Neier.

The Puzzle Palace: A Report on America's Most Secret Agency by James Bamford, Boston: Houghton Mifflin, 1982.

The only good exposé of the ultra-secret National Security Agency, which breaks laws all over the world, taps phones, and builds massive files on U.S. citizens.

Ropes of Sand: America's Failure in the Middle East by Wilbur Eveland, New York: Norton, 1980.

A former National Security Council officer's account of CIA/United States manipulations in the Middle East in the 1950s.

Secrecy and Democracy: The CIA in Transition by Stansfield Turner, Boston: Houghton Mifflin, 1985.

A former CIA Director advocates covert action at the expense of democratic freedoms.

The Spy Who Got Away: The Inside Story of Edward Lee Howard, the CIA Agent Who Betrayed His Country's Secrets and Escaped to Moscow by David Wise, New York: Random House, 1988.

A detailed account of Ed Howard, the CIA operative who was selected for a stressful assignment in the CIA's station in the U.S. Embassy in Moscow, despite drug and alcohol abuse problems. Fired, he delivered to the Soviets the identities of the CIA's network in Moscow. Under close surveillance by the FBI at his home in New Mexico, he managed to slip away and now lives under KGB protection in the Soviet Union.

The Ugly American by William J. Lederer and Eugene Burdick, New York: Norton, 1958.

This famous book was based on the lifestyle and activities of the CIA operative, Ed Lansdale, who bullied and manipulated events in the Philippines and then South Vietnam in the 1950s.

Under Cover: Thirty-Five Years of CIA Deception by Darrell Garwood, New York: Grove, 1985.

Another good summary of prominent CIA destabilizations, written by a journalist who was covering the Pentagon and CIA during many of those 35 years.

White Paper Whitewash: Interview with Philip Agee on the CIA and El Salvador, New York: Deep Cover Books, 1981.

Debunks the original "White Paper" that General Haig presented to the Congress, our allies, and then the public in 1981, supposedly proving Soviet/Cuban sponsorship of the FMLN in El Salvador. Haig was obliged to reappear before Congressional committees and admit that the Soviet "masterminds" named in the paper were fabricated.

Wilderness of Mirrors by David C. Martin, New York: Harper and Row, 1980.

Martin discusses one of the intelligence world's greatest ironies: Jim Angleton, the CIA's famous and very paranoid counter-intelligence chief suspected nearly everyone of being a Soviet agent except his own friend and mentor, Kim Philby, who was!

VII: ON KILLING AND MAKING U.S. PRESIDENTS

THE ASSASSINATION OF JOHN F. KENNEDY

Best Evidence: Disguise and Deception in the Assassination of John F. Kennedy by David S. Lifton, New York: Macmillan, 1980.

A detailed study of the extensive evidence that proves President Kennedy could not possibly have been killed by a lone assassin.

Betrayal by Robert D. Morrow, Chicago: H. Regnery, 1976.

A former contract officer of the CIA, involved in CIA activities to destabilize Cuba, reconstructs how a CIA team with Mafia contacts plotted the ambush and assassination of President Kennedy.

The Company: A Novel by John Ehrlichman, New York: Simon and Schuster, 1976.

Although fiction, this book's meaning is crystal clear, as the President (Nixon) is blackmailed by the CIA Director (Dick Helms) into dropping his efforts to find the file that would prove the CIA's involvement in the killing of President Kennedy.

Conspiracy by Anthony Summers, New York: Paragon House, 1989.

One of the best books written about the events surrounding the assassination of President Kennedy. There was a conspiracy; the CIA and organized crime were responsible, but Army intelligence, the FBI, and the Dallas Police also had prior knowledge and prior contact with the alleged killer and were permitted to destroy evidence of that contact and to lie to the Warren Commission.

However, Summers does not deal with the witnesses and potential whistleblowers who were killed during the cover-up and he does not project the logical conclusions. He accepts the assertion that one "Magic Bullet" could have passed through two men's bodies, clothes, and bones, and emerged miraculously undeformed.

Contract on America: The Mafia Murders of John and Robert Kennedy by David E. Scheim, Silver Spring, MD: Argyle Press, 1983.

Reviews the evidence that the killing of John Kennedy was engineered by the mob. Evidence of CIA involvement is conspicuously absent, and a lively debate rages between advocates of a mob conspiracy, and advocates of a CIA conspiracy in the Kennedy killing.

The Ends of Power by H.R. Haldeman with Joseph DiMona, New York: Times Books, 1978.

   Some useful further corroboration.

The Final Assassination Report of the Select Committee on Intelligence, U.S. House of Representatives, 1979.

   Although the investigation was politicized and continuously sabotaged by those who were determined to perpetuate the cover-up, it did at the last moment conclude that there *was* a conspiracy. With that conclusion one must ask how it is possible that the House did not pressure the Justice Department to appoint a special prosecutor to investigate.

Legend: The Secret World of Lee Harvey Oswald by Edward Jay Epstein, New York: Reader's Digest, 1978.

   This book advances the theory that the Soviets, desperate that the United States not conclude that the Soviet Union had programmed Lee Harvey Oswald to kill the U.S. President, arranged for a high-ranking KGB officer to defect with reassuring information. The officer, Yuri Nosenko, spent three years imprisoned in a CIA safehouse before he was "cleared" and thereafter used by the CIA in sensitive consulting roles.

On the Trail of Assassins: My Investigation and Prosecution of the Murder of President Kennedy by Jim Garrison, New York: Sheridan Square Press, 1988.

   This important book details New Orleans District Attorney Jim Garrison's frustrations in trying to bring the conspirators to justice only to be thwarted by the mysterious deaths of witnesses, government files that were closed to him, and vicious attacks by the media. Garrison does not address the power and influence of the Mafia in New Orleans and Dallas, or the evidence of its involvement in the assassination.

Reasonable Doubt: An Investigation into the Assassination of John F. Kennedy by Henry Hurt, New York: Holt, Rinehart, and Winston, 1986.

   In spite of abundant, dramatic evidence pointing to a conspiracy, Hurt feels that it is highly unlikely that we shall ever know the full truth of the assassination and cover-up.

The Senator Must Die by Robert D. Morrow, Santa Monica, CA:

Roundtable, 1988.

Morrow, author of *Betrayal,* reconstructs how President Kennedy was killed and silenced by the CIA and the Mafia, and presents compelling evidence of how the CIA, Mafia, and agents of the Iranian SAVAK also slew Robert Kennedy the night it became apparent that he would win the U.S. presidency in 1968. As with Oswald five years previously, law enforcement offices worked determinedly to blame the killing on a lone assassin, this time Sirhan Sirhan.

The Tears of Autumn by Charles McCarry, New York: Fawcet Crest, 1974.

A fictionalized account of the CIA-engineered *coup d'état* in Vietnam in which the premier, Ngo Dinh Diem, was killed in early November 1963. Two weeks later, according to this thesis, the Diem family took its revenge on the U.S. President.

Witness to Power: The Nixon Years by John Ehrlichman, New York: Simon and Schuster, 1982.

Offers evidence of background on the linkage between the CIA and the Mafia in the assassination business.

THE REAGAN REVOLUTION

Corruptions of Empire: Life Studies and the Reagan Era by Alexander Cockburn, New York: Verso, 1988.

A collection of Cockburn's penetrating columns that detail the Reagan revolution as no other work probably ever will.

The Iran-Contra Connection: Secret Teams and Covert Operations in the Reagan Era by Jane Hunter, Jonathan Marshall, and Peter Dale Scott, Boston: South End Press, 1987.

Remarkable in its timeliness, this book weaves the Iran/*contra* scandal into the fabric of the Reagan Revolution.

On Reagan: The Man and His Presidency by Ronnie Dugger, New York: McGraw-Hill, 1983.

This is a well-researched summary of Ronald Reagan's career. In the last chapter Dugger deals with Reagan's fixation on Armageddon.

Reagan's America by Lloyd deMause, New York: Creative

Roots, 1984.

A fascinating psycho-history that analyzes Reagan's obsession with military and political power as well as his very personal antipathy for people like Muammar Quadafi and Daniel Ortega, his willingness to engage them in personal name-calling, his craving to make them "cry uncle," and his exultation over bombing and invading countries like Libya and Grenada that are so weak they cannot be considered in terms of the world power structure.

The Secret Life of Ronald Reagan by Larry Flynt and Donald Freed, Hustler Press, 1984.

Ronald Reagan's character is further developed and his radical background exposed in this remarkably well-written book. The authors argue that Reagan never was "conservative." Throughout his career, he has been attracted to radical right-wing cabals, some of which advocated assassination, military takeover, and harsh repression of American society. One can only conclude that he and his backers were planning a quantum leap forward for the national security state under his administration.

The Triumph of Politics: How the Reagan Revolution Failed by David Stockman, New York: Harper and Row, 1986.

The chief witch doctor admits that Reagan's voodoo economics was doomed from the start and did irreparable damage to the U.S. economy.

VIII: LATIN AMERICA

Assassination on Embassy Row by John Dinges and Saul Landau, New York: Pantheon Books, 1980.

The U.S. government was embarrassed when its protegé, the military government of Chile (installed in the CIA destabilization/coup of 1972-73) and CIA operatives who were veterans of the Bay of Pigs, engineered a bombing on embassy row in our own capital. It was not, however embarrassed enough to hold Pinochet or DINA, his intelligence service, accountable.

Bitter Fruit: The Untold Story of the American Coup in Guatemala by Stephen Schlesinger and Stephen Kinzer, New York: Doubleday, 1982.

Secretary of State John Foster Dulles, his brother, CIA Director Allen Dulles, and Assistant Secretary of State for Inter-American Affairs John Lodge all had personal financial interests in the United Fruit Company and President Eisenhower's personal secretary was the public relations officer for United Fruit. Guatemalan President Jacobo Arbenz was trying to buy back unused lands from United Fruit to distribute in a land reform program. Arbenz was labelled a "Communist" and the CIA organized an invasion force and removed him from power in 1954. Since the ouster, hopes for land and social reform have faded into distant memories as successive repressive regimes have slaughtered over 100,000 Guatemalan peasants, mostly Mayan Indians.

Closest of Enemies: A Personal and Diplomatic Account of U.S.-Cuban Relations Since 1957 by Wayne S. Smith, New York: Norton, 1987.

Smith served for twenty-odd years with the Department of State, specializing in Cuban affairs. In 1982, he resigned in protest over President Reagan's policies toward Cuba. This book documents the numerous times the United States rejected opportunities to improve relations with Cuba. An excellent book, but Smith makes no serious effort to discuss the CIA's destabilization of Cuba or the operations that he personally "covered" for as chief of the U.S. Interest Section in Havana. Also, the chapter on Angola contains some minor chronological errors that were corrected in the paperback.

Contra Terror in Nicaragua: A Report of the Fact-Finding Mission, September 1984-January 1985 by Reed Brody, Boston: South End Press, 1985.

Brody, a former assistant attorney general of New York state, meticulously documents *contra* atrocities in Nicaragua.

Demonstration Elections: U.S.-Staged Elections in the Dominican Republic, Vietnam, and El Salvador by Edward S. Herman and Frank Brodhead, Boston: South End Press, 1984.

The U.S. government's definition of Third World democracy is elections that are bought and manipulated by the CIA.

El Salvador: Central America in the New Cold War by Marvin E. Gettleman, Patrick Lacefield, Louis Menashe, and David Marmelstein, New York: Grove, 1987.

The horror and anguish continue, with substantial subsidies by the United States. The U.S. establishment works in two basic ways in its efforts to control Third World countries: one is destabilization, as in the case of Nicaragua throughout the 1980s, and the other is the installation and support of repressive institutions like the death squads in El Salvador.

El Salvador: The Face of Revolution by Robert Armstrong and Janet Shenk, Boston: South End Press, 1982.

An excellent book on revolution. It measures the tolerance of a people who are gradually, through decades of brutal repression, driven to rise up.

See also the outstanding films, *Salvador* by Oliver Stone and *The Mission* by Roland Joffe.

The Fish Is Red: The Story of the Secret War Against Castro by Warren Hinckle and William W. Turner, New York: Harper and Row, 1981.

For several long years, the CIA attacked Cuba with a secret army, much like the Nicaraguan *contras,* based in Florida. It introduced sabotage teams into Cuba, burned sugarcane crops, planted bombs in department stores, disseminated a plague of swine fever, and murdered and raped. The result backfired, serving to consolidate the Cuban revolution behind Castro. Eventually, President Kennedy was killed and the new President, Lyndon Johnson, succeeded in retargeting the CIA elsewhere.

See also the CBS and PBS documentaries by Walter Cronkite, Dan Rather, and Bill Moyers.

Hidden Terrors by A.J. Langguth, New York: Pantheon, 1978.

This book describes the torture programs of the Office of Public Safety, mostly in Latin American, that are discussed in detail in the above text.

See also the films, *On Company Business* by Alan Francovich and *State of Siege* by Costa Gavras.

Labyrinth by Taylor Branch and Eugene M. Proper, New York: Viking, 1982.

Taylor Branch, who "ghosted" John Dean's book about Watergate, teams up with the district attorney who prosecuted the men who were responsible for bombing Orlando Letelier's car on embassy row in Washington, DC.

Missing: The Execution of Charles Horman: An American Sacrifice by Thomas Hauser, New York: Simon and Schuster, 1988.

The CIA mounted an operation to oust President Salvador Allende and terminate constitutional democracy in Chile. Many people were executed, including an American, Charles Horman. This story was put to film by Costa Gavras in a film with the same title, starring Jack Leman and David Clennon.

Nicaragua: The Sandinista Revolution by Henri Weber, trans. Patrick Cammiler, New York: Verso, 1981.

See also the documentary film, *Destination Nicaragua* by Barbara Trent and David Kaspar, and Haskel Wexler's film, *Latino.*

The Open Veins of Latin America by Eduardo Galeano, New York: Monthly Review Press, 1973.

An all-time classic.

See also the film, *When Mountains Tremble,* for passionate representations of the suffering and dying peoples of Latin America.

Washington's War on Nicaragua by Holly Sklar, Boston: South End Press, 1988.

An excellent detailed summation of this sad and reprehensible chapter of U.S. aggression, propaganda, and manipulation.

With the Contras: A Reporter in the Wilds of Nicaragua by Christopher Dickey, New York: Simon and Schuster, 1987.

A "middle of the road" journalist for the *Washington Post* and *Newsweek,* Dickey went on patrol with the *contras* and gives a fascinating glimpse into the brutal madness of the leaders. His credibility in presenting this account is perversely enhanced by his expression of "deep sympathy for the men and women of the CIA" in the foreword. Nowhere in his book does he explicitly express his sympathy for the CIA's victims.

IX: SOUTHEAST ASIA

A Bright Shining Lie: John Paul Vann and America in Vietnam by Neil Sheehan, New York: Vintage, 1989.

Eighteen years in the writing, this detailed, honest, and perceptive account treats the U.S. adventure in Vietnam through the experience of John Vann, who was there throughout the critical years of 1962-1972. This is unquestionably one of the two or three most important books that have been written about the Vietnam War in spite of its length.

Born on the Fourth of July by Ron Kovic, New York: Pocket Books, 1977.

Rendered paraplegic in Vietnam, a super-patriot at last *understands.* Director Oliver Stone and actor Tom Cruise made this book into an award-winning movie.

Cover-Up: The Army's Secret Investigation of the Massacre at My Lai by Seymour Hersh, New York: Random House, 1972.

About the infamous massacre at My Lai, in Vietnam.

Fire in the Lake: The Vietnamese and the Americans in Vietnam by Frances Fitzgerald, New York: Vintage, 1973.

This book, written by the daughter of the CIA's infamous Deputy Director of operations, Desmond Fitzgerald, highlighted the anti-Vietnam War effort.

Kiss the Boys Goodbye by Monika Jensen Stevenson and William Stevenson, New York: Penguin, 1990.

A former prize-winning "60-Minutes" producer and her husband, also the author of *A Man Called Intrepid*, write this definitive, compelling book about U.S. prisoners of war who were abandoned by the United States at the end of the Vietnam War. Drafted and recruited, sent to fight the Vietnam War with all its sideshows, hundreds of American soldiers were left behind as abandoned prisoners of war in the U.S. "honorable" withdrawal in the mid-1970s. Politicians and the national security establishment worked tirelessly to deny their existence and discourage loved ones from finding and freeing them.

A Nation Betrayed by Bo Gritz, Boulder City, Nevada: Lazarus, 1988.

The United States' most decorated Green Beret commander from the Vietnam War recounts how he undertook hazardous missions into postwar Laos to find MIAs, only to discover that high U.S. officials were deeply involved in the drug trade and willfully leaving U.S. soldiers forgotten prisoners in the Southeast Asian jungles.

The Pentagon Papers by Neil Sheehan, Hedrick Smith, E.W. Kenworth, and Fox Butterfield, New York: Bantam Books, 1971.

These authentic papers, made public by Daniel Ellsberg, prove the incident in the Bay of Tonkin that was used to trigger the U.S. invasion of Vietnam was a fraud and illustrate a systematic pattern of lying by government officials to the U.S. public.

The Perfect War: Technowar in Vietnam by James William Gibson, Boston: Atlantic Monthly Press, 1986.

If you only have time to read one book about Vietnam, it should be this one.

The PHOENIX Program by Douglas Valentine, New York: Morrow, 1990.

At last we have a thorough exposé of the infamous PHOENIX "counter-terrorist" program, which its own Director, eventual CIA Director William Colby, acknowledged killed over 20,000 people. The book details the computerized assassination and torture program in which citizens as well as "enemy" were brutally killed.

Saigon by Anthony Grey, New York: Simon and Schuster, 1982.

Fiction—an easy way to absorb the history of events in Vietnam, 1925-1975.

Tet! by Don Oberdorfer, New York: Doubleday, 1971.

A journalist's account of the 1968 Viet Cong offensive that

was the turning point of the war.

CBS Special on General Westmoreland by Mike Wallace and "60 Minutes"/CBS, New York, 1981.

An exposé of the body count game of the Vietnam War: the gross exaggeration of our "success" in Vietnam to justify Westmoreland's expansion of the war. (Westmoreland sued 60 MINUTES and lost resoundingly.)

The Thirteenth Valley: A Novel by John M. Del Vecchio, New York: Bantam, 1982.

Fiction. This is the *Naked and the Dead* of the Vietnam War.

The Tunnels of Cu Chi by Tom Mangold and John Penycate, New York: Random House, 1985.

The incredible story of the Viet Cong tunnels, hundreds of kilometers of them, and of the lives and determination of the people who dug them a handful of dirt at a time and then lived for five and ten years beneath the ground. (When I returned to Vietnam in 1985, I discovered that some of the tunnels had been opened for tourists. I was able to stand, peering out of a spider-hole at the roads we once drove daily in my CIA activities. It was only by grace of Hanoi's policies not to knock off American officials that we survived the experience.)

A Vietcong Memoir by Troung Nhu Tang with David Chanoff and Doan Van Toai, New York: Vintage, 1986.

The partisan account of the highest ranking Vietcong official in exile from Vietnam.

Vietnam: A History by Stanley Karnow, New York: Penguin, 1984.

This is the first formal history of our Vietnam War, useful but limited. Karnow gives only passing mention of the CIA's prominent role in dragging the United States into the war. It therefore qualifies as the stylized, official history and cover story for the Vietnam War.

365 Days by Ronald J. Glasser, New York: Braziller, 1981.

The best book I've found about soldiers, who are the second victims of any war. The first victim is of course the *truth*. Third, more tragic and more obvious, are the innocent civilians who inevitably die in greater numbers, with less care and support, than the soldiers.

X: MIDDLE EAST AND AFRICA

The Eagle and the Lion: The Tragedy of American-Iranian Relations by James Bill, New Haven: Yale University Press, 1988.

A useful but far from comprehensive history, which touches on many, but not all of the misunderstandings and tragedies that have occurred in official United States/Iran relations. The book does not report on former CIA Director, Richard Helms, who became ambassador to Iran, then joined the Shah's payroll and declared himself an agent of a foreign government after retiring. The author uses the word "CIA" as seldom as possible, despite the organization's well-documented, extensive involvement in the ouster of the democratically elected leader, Mossadeq, the installation of the Shah, and the creation of the dreaded SAVAK, or secret police.

The Fateful Triangle: The United States, Israel and the Palestinians by Noam Chomsky, Boston: South End Press, 1983.

A compelling, no-punches-pulled analysis of the Israel/Palestine/United States connection, this book strikes sparks.

The Tragedy of Afghanistan: A Firsthand Account by Raja Anwar, New York: Verso, 1988.

The Soviets withdrew their troops and most of the world applauded, but millions have been killed or dislocated, the country remains a battlefield, and the region has become the world's richest source of heroin smuggling.

Long forgotten in all the propaganda and disinformation is the fact that the Soviet invasion was precipitated by the CIA's destabilization and attempted *coup d'état* in the late 1970s. (Other CIA destabilizations provoked the Soviets to put their armies into Czechoslovakia in 1968 and Hungary in 1956.)

Y Victoria: Hidden Lives, Hidden Deaths; South Africa's Crippling of a Continent by Victoria Britain, London: Faber and Faber, 1988.

Out of sight, out of mind: by shutting off western media access, South Africa has been able to continue to run rampant, bombing and pillaging its neighbors like 20th-century Huns.

XI: "FRATERNAL" ORGANIZATIONS

Agents of Repression: The FBI's Secret Wars Against the Black Panther Party and the American Indian Movement by Ward Churchill and Jim Vander Wall, Boston: South End Press, 1990.

By Way of Deception: The Making and Unmaking of a Mossad Officer by Victor Ostrovsky with Claire Hoy, New York: St. Martins, 1990.

This perhaps is the starkest view inside any intelligence service. Victor Ostrovsky lays open Israel's Mossad, which inside the intelligence world, is thought to be the most effective (perhaps because of its ruthlessness) of all the services. Its secrecy covers cynical operations against its allies, the training of brutal, repressive police services such as in South Africa and Idi Amin's Uganda, unbridled arms dealings, blackmailing its own citizens, sacrificing its own agents, and considerable in-house sexual activity. Understandably, Mossad fought desperately to block the publication of this book.

The CIA-Mafia Link by Charles Ashman, New York: Manor Books, 1975.

The title speaks for itself. The CIA and the Mafia are natural allies.

The COINTELPRO Papers: Documents from the FBI's Secret Wars Against Dissent in the United States by Ward Churchill and Jim Vander Wall, Boston: South End Press, 1990.

Conspiracy of Silence by Anthony Pearson, New York: Quartet, 1978.

U.S. intelligence chiefs cooperated with Israel's Mossad to cover up the Israeli attack on the USS *Liberty*, in which CIA employees and U.S. servicemen were killed.

Deep Cover: An FBI Agent Infiltrates the Radical Underground by Cril Payne, New York: Newsweek Press, 1979.

    About the FBI.

Endless Enemies: The Making of an Unfriendly World by Jonathan Kwitny, New York: Congdon and Weed, 1984.

    Our banks have loaned and continue to loan countries more money than they can ever repay. Why permit dictators like the Shah, Ferdinand Marcos, Mobutu Sese Seko, Anastasio Somoza, and their cohorts to steal billions of dollars? Kwitny, a *Wall Street Journal* reporter at the time he wrote this book, provides the clearest explanation I have ever read.

The Great Heroin Coup: Drugs, Intelligence, and International Fascism by Henrik Krüger, Boston: South End Press, 1980.

    CIA and White House involvement as international organized crime shifted its operations from France to Southeast Asia.

The Hidden World of Interpol by Omar Garrison, New York: Rolston Pilot, 1976.

    The title speaks for itself.

In Banks We Trust by Penny Lernoux, New York: Penguin, 1986.

    We are conditioned to see our banking institutions as sober and conservative, yet in the real world they speculate, bungle, and steal. In fact, even the biggest banks are now teetering on the edge of collapse as a result of greed, mismanagement, and the granting of irrecoverable international loans.

INFACT Brings GE to Light by INFACT, 1988 (INFACT, P.O. Box 3223, South Pasadena, CA, 91031).

    General Electric, Ronald Reagan's historic employer and benefactor, and a giant multinational "defense" corporation that also owns NBC, has for two decades been bulldozing opposition to its B-1 bomber program which, although enormously profitable for the manufacturer, was obsolete before it came off the drawing boards.

Inside BOSS: South Africa's Secret Police by Gordon Winter, London: Allen Lane, 1981.

A misnamed book because its author was not exactly "inside" the notorious South African secret service. He was an outside contract agent. Nevertheless, it is a useful exposé.

Israeli Foreign Policy: South Africa and Central America by Jane Hunter, Boston: South End Press, 1987.

Israel works as the U.S. proxy while advancing its own interests and a harsh right-wing agenda abroad: neutralizing the isolation of South Africa, bolstering repressive regimes in Guatemala, El Salvador, and Honduras, aiding the Nicaraguan *contras,* and inhibiting Costa Rica's aspirations of neutrality.

The Killing of Karen Silkwood: The Story Behind the Kerr McGee Plutonium Case by Richard L. Rashke, Boston: Houghton Mifflin, 1981.

For trying to tell the truth about radiation poisoning, Karen Silkwood was murdered. The FBI and NSA were involved in this unpunished crime, which may symbolize the future of free speech in the national security state.

Kim Philby, The Spy I Loved by Eleanor Philby, London: Pam Books, 1967.

The Director of the British Service was a Russian spy during his entire career! Yes, that means that every British intelligence operation, and many of the CIA's were known to the Russians.

The Media Monopoly, third edition, by Ben H. Bagdikian, Boston: Beacon Press, 1990.

Bagdikian documents the financial interrelationships between the media giants and the leading defense contractors. A dozen of the men who sit on the board of the *New York Times* and CBS also sit on the boards of 26 other multi-national corporations and defense contractors. NBC, for example, is owned by General Electric.

Secrecy and Power: The Life of J. Edgar Hoover by Richard Gid Powers, New York: Free Press, 1987.

Deemed "the best biography of Hoover so far" by the *New York Times*, this book pulls its punches. It does not deal with Hoover's policy of blackmailing colleagues, U.S. Representatives, and Senators if they stood in his way or threatened to investigate the FBI, which he virtually created. Nor does it mention the personal corruption, or the $900,000 government auditors found Hoover had stolen from the public when they audited his estate after his death. Although the revered founder and long-time chief of the FBI persistently denied that organized crime was a problem in U.S. society, he accepted free vacations from Mafia figures. This biographical information makes it much easier to understand the FBI's conduct in launching the cover-up of the Kennedy assassination.

Spooks: The Haunting of America: The Private Use of Secret Agents by Jim Hougan, New York: Morrow, 1978.

About industrial intelligence operatives.

Switzerland Exposed by Jean Ziegler, trans. Rosemary Middleton, London: Allison and Busby, 1978.

Switzerland, famous for its military neutrality, is one of the greediest in exploiting the Third World.

Veil: The Secret Wars of the CIA 1981-1987 by Bob Woodward, New York: Simon and Schuster, 1987.

While fascinating and important, Woodward takes too much license in reconstructing dialogue that was not recorded and which he did not personally witness. In addition, his inattention to specific dates of events further reduces the book's value as a history. His interpretation of CIA Director William Casey's conduct of office is nevertheless an important contribution to our understanding of the excesses of the Reagan Revolution.

Perhaps most important, however, is the book's revelation of the intimate relationship that exists between the CIA and the *Washington Post*. Every time the *Post* did a story about the CIA, its editors faithfully called the CIA Director to clear it *vis à vis* "national security." This symbiotic relationship between the *Post* and the CIA is no great secret, nor is it the first time *Post* insiders have acknowledged it. In fact, in 1981, as President Reagan was bringing his radical "revolution" into the White House, Katherine Graham, the owner of the *Washington Post* and *Newsweek,* announced at a press conference that her editors "would cooperate with national security (CIA) interests." *Veil* reveals that she intervened at one point on behalf of CIA Director Casey, at the personal request of Ronald Reagan.

War at Home: Covert Action Against U.S. Activists and What We Can Do About It by Brian Glick, Boston: South End Press, 1989.

XII: MIND CONTROL

Acid Dreams: The CIA, LSD, and the Sixties Rebellion by Martin A. Lee and Bruce Shlain, New York: Grove, 1985.

Pseudoscientists in the CIA, playing with hallucinogens, scarcely bothering to keep records, experimented on the American public and then launched a crusade to push LSD into the society at large.

Clouds of Secrecy: The Army's Germ Warfare Tests Over Populated Areas by Leonard A. Cole, Totowa, NJ: Rowman and Littlefield, 1988.

A succinct account of the U.S. Army's past and continuing experimentation on U.S. population centers with toxic materials.

The Cocaine Wars by Paul Eddy, Hugo Sabogal, and Sara Walden, New York: Norton, 1988.

"Miami Vice" is not fiction!

The Mind Manipulators by Alan W. Shiflin and Edward M. Opton, New York: Paddington, 1978.

Operation Mind Control by W. H. Bowart, New York: Dell, 1978.

The Search for the "Manchurian Candidate": The CIA and Mind Control by John Marks, New York: Times Books, 1979.

Based on 14,000 documents obtained from the CIA under the Freedom of Information Act, this book details the CIA's 20-year experimentation on American citizens with various chemicals and techniques of mind control.

XIII: A DARK HOUR

Naming Names by Victor S. Navasky, New York: Viking, 1990.
   In the early 1950s, a xenophobic craze swept the country.
People were harassed, fired, jailed, and even executed before
sanity was restored. Today, the national security complex is
moving somewhat more quietly as it pursues the same objectives, muzzling and discrediting its enemies and gaining un-
shakable control of American society.

On Doing Time by Morton Sobell, New York: Scribner's, 1974.
   Convicted with Julius and Ethel Rosenberg, Sobel served
19 years in maximum security prisons.

We Are Your Sons: The Legacy of Ethel and Julius Rosenberg by
Robert and Michael Meeropol, Urbana: University of Illinois
Press, 1986.
   The legacy of Julius and Ethel Rosenberg, written by their
sons. The parents were convicted of espionage and electrocuted,
and 20 years later documents obtained under the Freedom of
Information Act reveal that J. Edgar Hoover himself did not
believe the mother was guilty. In the light of history, the evidence against Julius is not persuasive either.

XIV: OTHER COUNTRIES, OTHER VIEWS

Armageddon in Prime Time by George Bailey, New York: Avon,
1984.
   An ABC correspondent's summary of the U.S. rivalry with
the Soviet Union. Bailey makes the point that the Soviet economy has produced nothing "aside from vodka and caviar" that
anyone is eager to buy.

*Congo Cables: The Cold War in Africa—From Eisenhower to
Kennedy* by Madeleine G. Kalb, New York: Macmillan, 1982.
   A remarkable illustration of our limited perceptions of
world events. Kalb spent a number of years in Moscow with her
husband, who was on assignment for the *New York Times*. In
this book, she presents the clearest account of Soviet Premier

Nikita Khrushchev's frustrations over his inability to stand up to the United States in the Congo (now Zaire) in the early 1960s. This was the circumstance that led to his pounding on a table with his shoe at the United Nations. Like Stanley Karnow, Kalb is a member of the establishment press. The "cables" on which she bases her account are State Department cables. She did not have access to the CIA cables and scarcely mentions its dominant role in the birthing of that important African nation.

It is also worth noting that this book about a black African country, highly acclaimed by various prominent media figures is startlingly insensitive, actually recounting ethnic and (male) chauvinist anecdotes.

The First Circle by Alexander Solzhenitsyn, trans. Michael Guybon, London: Fontana, 1979.

The author is a Soviet who loves his country and deplores the Stalinist abuses of those in power.

Honorable Men: My Life in the CIA by William Colby and Peter Forbath, New York: Simon and Schuster, 1978.

A former CIA Director's ghost-written *apologia*. In retirement, Colby continues to trumpet CIA disinformation.

A Key to Africa by Kenneth Bridgeland, London: Coronet Books, 1986.

If this is not an example of "grey" propaganda (i.e., secretly encouraged by some government), then it is a straightforward effort by a conservative journalist to promote Jonas Savimbi, who was feted by the Reagan White House and is, by admission of the U.S. government, receiving military support from the CIA. Savimbi openly asserts his personal friendship with white South African leaders and has admitted receiving military aid from South Africa. The author, by the way, admitted in a television interview to having been the vehicle of CIA propaganda about Jonas Savimbi into the media during the Angolan covert action of 1975.

The KGB Today: The Hidden Hand by John Barron, New York: Reader's Digest, 1983.

An arch-conservative's account. Barron admits to receiving help from a KGB defector who almost certainly remains on the

CIA payroll.

Land of the Firebird: The Beauty of Old Russia by Suzanne Massie, New York: Simon and Schuster, 1980.

This is the book that President Reagan claimed to have read, and recommended, about the Soviet Union.

Nicaragua, Revolution in the Family by Shirley Christian, New York: Random House, 1985.

Recommended by the State Department and the U.S. embassy in Managua. Need I say more?

The Russians by Hedrick Smith, New York: Ballantine Books, 1984.

A respected *New York Times* journalist's observations about the Soviet Union of the Cold War era.

The Spike by Arnaud de Borchgrave and Robert Moss, New York: Crown, 1980.

Fiction, and an unapologetic effort to discredit the American left as part of the Communist conspiracy, by two journalists who make no secret of their sympathy for the CIA.

The Terror Network: The Secret War of International Terrorism by Claire Sterling, New York: Berkeley Books, 1982.

Written as a propaganda piece to blame the Soviet Union for international terrorism, this work was taken up as the Bible of the conservative advocates of "national security." A small embarrassment to them was the fact that both the CIA's and the FBI's studies of the subject concluded that the Soviet Union was *not* responsible for terrorist activities that affected the United States. Their solution? The CIA Director, William Casey, ordered the CIA's reports to be rewritten to conform with Sterling's propaganda work. Such is the "intelligence" that U.S. taxpayers are underwriting to the tune of several billion dollars per year.

Index

About South End Press

South End Press is a nonprofit, collectively run book publisher with over 150 titles in print. Since our founding in 1977, we have tried to meet the needs of readers who are exploring, or are already committed to, the politics of radical social change.

Our goal is to publish books that encourage critical thinking and constructive action on the key political, cultural, social, economic, and ecological issues shaping life in the United States and in the world. In this way, we hope to give expression to a wide diversity of democratic social movements and to provide an alternative to the products of corporate publishing.

If you would like a free catalog of South End Press books or information about our membership program—which offers two free books and a 40% discount on all titles—please write us at South End Press, 116 Saint Botolph Street, Boston, MA 02115.

Other titles of interest from South End Press:

Necessary Illusions, Thought Control in Democratic Societies
Noam Chomsky

Culture of Terrorism
Noam Chomsky

Freedom Under Fire, U.S. Civil Liberties in Times of War
Michael Linfield

The Sun Never Sets
Confronting the Network of Foreign Military Bases
Edited by Joe Gerson and Bruce Birchard

The U.S. Invasion of Panama
The Independent Commission of Inquiry on the
U.S. Invasion of Panama

Walking to the Edge, Essays of Resistance
Margaret Randall